Christmas Abiding

Stories of Blessings Bestowed

James B. Macomson, DDS
Illustrated by Audrey McDonald

ISBN: 978-1-7339945-1-4

Published by Warren Publishing
Charlotte, NC
www.warrenpublishing.net
Printed in the United States

Profits from this book will be donated to charities.

Dedicated to you, the reader

TABLE OF CONTENTS

ACKNOWLEDGMENTS

"Thanks" is a word used universally by all, for so much. It is to give credit and appreciation and recognize the acts of one, or of many. The writing and publishing of a book cannot be done alone by the one holding the pen; the "supporting engineers" whose specialty is the proper construction and finishing of the project are vital; they are the ones closest to it. To Mindy, Amy, Audrey, Jere, and Kay, you know—merci, gracias, danke. Thank you for your tolerance, understanding, and acceptance beyond the writing. And to my family, friends, and the unknown ones, my hope is that a deeper appreciation comes through reading some of the many universal messages of Christmas.

Finally, let us all give thanks to Christmas and to the One who through His Grace and Love gave everything: our one God.

By Lantern's Light

ELECTRICITY. It ended as the mountains began their rise; a junction that separated the present and the past ... cultures. To civilization came power generated from the river of those mountains: energy—once early conveniences, now necessities. Telephones followed, cranked by their users—connections from the small town to larger and more progressive places they were. Civilization was hindered by geography and not by the inhabitants who lived in those different locations. They congenially coexisted, albeit sporadically, with manifested self-imposed societal distances.

Saturdays brought those of the mountains and those of the town together at the town's open market. Buying, selling, and bartering were the methods of exchange; ham and bacon for needles and thread, logs of oak and eggs for kerosene and soap, handmade quilts for shoes, and coffee for moonshine. Of this, the constable frowned, but then with a smile and nod, looked away. These interactions rendered a slow and better understanding of each other; encounters of lives, not just people.

The children. Through the developing knowledge of changing times, all knew theirs was the epicenter of human progress: growth and betterment. The school. Those closest to it walked. Further away, some were brought down the mountain roads by horse and wagon. But there were others who lived too far, making the distances not simply impractical, but impossible. Reading, writing, and simple mathematics were more than objectives, they were essential requirements to adapt, reshape, and transform—all part of the upward evolution of their very being. They possessed few barriers, these school children—any incongruence of dress or speech was overcome by stern instructions from parents. Together they learned, ate, and played, Mondays through Fridays. They parted weekends and summers, but every Saturday they could be seen, separate from parents, together at that market doing what children did best—being children.

The Saturdays in December, the market's activities increased as Christmas approached. The first occurrence that signaled the coming holidays were the trees: fir, balsam, and cedar were cut and brought from the highest reaches of the mountains. Stacked high in the long wagons, mules that loped and lingered easily pulled those seasonal treasures. Something else happened during those days: no money was seen. Unspoken by any, it was the season of giving. It happened with these two different cultures, the exchanging of gifts unique only to themselves, one to another—of the mountains, of the town. But of question and concern, someone who always came was missing....

Five miles up the first mountain lay a man on a bed, the man who organized, delegated, and directed the harvesting of those trees. His name was Jedediah. "Jed" had a leg broken when a loaded wagon tipped over on him. The town doctor had gone to treat and set that leg, as he had done for many people after accidents of broken limbs. The doctor left Jed, his leg set securely between two flat pine planks. Relief from the pain came from the doctor's prescription: every four hours, four ounces of moonshine. It always worked. Nothing was heard from Jed's family until the evening— two days before Christmas. He had taken "a turn for the worse." A fever. Delirium. News no one wanted.

Christmas Eve morning, the doctor and the minister—just in the event of the worst possibility—would go. The winding road was beginning to lose its definition as the falling snow covered it, but the two in the old car, with tires fit for the elements, had made the journey many times before and were not concerned. Halfway through the journey, the car lost its traction and slid into a deep rut. Prepared through past experience, the two got out and opened the trunk; a shovel and a bag of sand always with the spare tire were there. They began the familiar process—digging, shoveling away the snow, and proper placement of the sand; back-and-forth the car would rock. In the past happenings, their efforts had always been successful, but now these efforts yielded frustrations. Hours passed; morning was becoming afternoon. As darkness quickly approached, they could not walk the distance to the suffering Jed. A regrettable and agonizing decision they had to make—to return to the town. It would take only take two hours; they were dressed warmly and could follow the deep tire tracks. The doctor retrieved his medical bag; the minister, his Bible. Shutting the trunk and the doors of the car, they started down the long hill.

Then they saw it: far across and around the gentle curve of the hills leading down to a stream were beams of light shining through the leafless trees. The people of the town, they thought, realizing the conditions, had come to help. The two waited. It was not many, but only one light they saw. Rounding the turn at the bottom of the hill, the light began to dim. Coming into view, they saw only a single wagon being drawn by two massive mules. Although the light's brilliance lessened, it outlined the lone figure holding the reins. A man at such a distance they did not recognize, although in appearance, resembled the people of this locale.

Responding to their driver, the blanket-covered mules came to a shuffling stop. Having tied the leather reins to the wagon and viewing the dire predicament, he reached up to the metal pole to retrieve the lantern. It was metal framed with glass sides and a hinged door that enclosed a candle. The minister looked closely at it. It was different; simple in design and function but exhibiting resplendence almost sovereign in its material and making. He had seen similar ones in photographs and painted depictions from cathedrals and grand churches. The frame, not tarnished as brass, but gold it was. The glass: no imperfections were seen and with the clarity of the finest cut diamonds, it was almost invisible. The candle burned without a flicker; no wisps of smoke and without remains of melting wax.

As the stranger with his lantern looked at the failed efforts to free the car, the doctor told of the reasons for their journey, and with it already being dark and the snow deepening, how they could not reach their destination before the critical situation became fatal. The stranger motioned the two into the wagon—they would not just try but would continue up the mountain.

An hour later, leaving the main road, a two-lane path led to the house. Light came from the sole front window; smoke rose from the chimney. This house was isolated, as all were throughout the mountains. The house was made of logs and hand-hewn boards, and the roof was covered in an overlapping pattern of cedar shingles. Inside, the three men saw a large room with a ladder leading to a loft—an open area where the children slept. One wall of that room was a large rock fireplace with a pot hanging from an iron stand in its corner. A stack of logs lay in waiting next to the fireplace.

Jed's wife and two sons welcomed and thanked the three. She knew the doctor and the minister, but when she saw the stranger, with the meeting of their eyes, her hand covered her mouth. Saying nothing, she reached out and touched his hand holding the lantern. She motioned the three to the far end of the room and pulling back a curtain, they saw in its darkened corner, a bed. On it lay a motionless body, with the broken leg elevated beneath a quilt. Asking the stranger to bring his light closer, the doctor began his examination—the lantern beamed brighter. The light revealed immediately to the doctor how serious this situation was. Softly calling his name, no response came from Jed except the obvious pain as heard through his intermittent groans and grimaces. Surveying and processing what was seen, the doctor instantly knew the state of this man; an infection had begun at the fracture site and had spread throughout his body. Fever. The worst sign was the body's signaling of the fight it was now losing.

Lifting the quilt, they saw one of the bindings on the wooden splint had become twisted, caused by Jed's turning movements as he sought comfort. The temporary relief had caused strangulation of the body's vital vessels. Not speaking, the doctor quickly began the delicate task. A scream came from Jed, jolting everyone as he reacted to the untying of the strips of cloth that held the wooden splint. Reaching into his bag, the doctor retrieved a small glass bottle. Opening it, he poured it into Jed's mouth. There was a cough after the liquid was swallowed—morphine. The same as used on the fields of war to kill the agony of bombs and bullets, but here—bacteria. Minutes passed; Jed began to relax, then became motionless. The doctor's hands began orchestrated movements—removing, cleaning, replacing, realigning, and neatly fixing the new supports. The interrupted supply of life, blood, was restored.

Reaching back into his bag, he brought forth a glass syringe with a needle attached to it, which was inserted into a small bottle containing a milky white liquid—penicillin. Newly discovered, it was a miraculous enemy of infections. He filled the syringe and plunged it deep into Jed's muscular thigh. Jed's family gasped—vocal mistrust, without words; controlled respect with objection to modern medicine came from many of the back woods.

As the doctor finished the bandages and bindings and was about to cover the leg, Jed's wife asked if she could apply some of the "healing salve" that was made in these mountains. When he smiled and nodded yes, she gently smoothed some of the thick paste onto Jed's leg and a small amount on his fever-struck forehead. The doctor knew that the infection was throughout this man's body, and medically, this mix, whatever power it possessed, was only topical in its effects. In the past, he had seen it used in times like this when these people refused his aid and treatments. And many times he had received the news that the sick or wounded upon whom this natural remedy had been used did not survive.

Wanting one last look to survey and inspect, the doctor asked the stranger to bring his lantern closer to the damaged leg. As he lowered the light, from inside the crystalline glass of the lantern began to slowly haze, to fog, as was the natural reaction of cold air encountering heat. When the lantern now oddly became dimmer, the stranger reached and opened its tightly fitting door. Immediately it became brighter and a small wisp of vapor emerged and disappeared over the fractured leg—with it, an aroma of cinnamon and ginger ... Christmas.

Sitting at the bedside, the doctor's vigil continued. Leaving and pulling the curtain aside, the others went into the large room and sat. Voices muffled, they drank hot sassafras tea prepared in the pot that hung in the corner of the fireplace. The lantern sat on the table of smooth planks, adding a soft glow to that place.

Just before midnight, a groan was heard coming from behind the curtain. Quietly and quickly they all gathered around the bed with the quilt pulled to Jed's waist. They saw his night shirt was soaked with sweat as the doctor was drying his glistening wet face. The raging fever had broken....

Opening his pocket watch, the minister looked at the hands on its face: both were pointing to twelve midnight. The stranger held the lantern higher above his head; it began to glow brighter and brighter, giving a radiating brilliance to that small home. Turning, he walked toward the door. Putting on his great coat, scarf, hat, and gloves, he stopped and smiling, said "Merry Christmas." Outside, climbing into his wagon, he told them he lived on the far side of

the mountain and needed to get to his home; there were newborn lambs that liked to wander....

They all watched on that cold, star-filled night as the wagon slowly went up the long hill, to the top of the mountain—the lantern guiding its path. The minister began to speak:

And there were in the same country shepherds abiding in the field, keeping watch over their flock by night. And, lo, the Angel of the Lord came upon them and the glory of the Lord shone round about them....

It came before on the first Christmas Eve, and now, to a small part of a troubled world, from that lantern, The Light burned and would forevermore.

The Pen and the Rose

SUMMA CUM LAUDE: "With highest praise," from the Latin, these bold words were written just below her name. Academic adoration. Her diploma, a representation of four years of labors and study at a respected and revered university, was carefully wrapped and packed. It would travel. A passport not for entry into foreign lands, but a document to display to all where she had been—her passage ... a certificate of official issue that told more than what was written on it. It was implicit of accomplishment and more—potential.

Four months after graduation, by rail, the Pullman, for two days, carried her eastward. A private compartment. A fold-down bed. A place of privilege. A place of independence. A place usually consigned to those of wealth. An "expense" was this journey given by "them" … those who as the butterflies of spring seek the brightest of flowers. And just as this miracle of nature, they would do the same, but as an act of man … a human symbiosis.

They were the hunters and gatherers, those who sought success through discovery of that which nourished their very existence: people. Together, she and they would create a relationship of giving and receiving, yielding benefit to both. They knew of her, her history and education; it was far greater than "English Literature," the designation on that diploma. They also knew, with interest beyond acute, of that which she left behind—a book. It later, would also travel. In reverse it began. Not gliding and floating, the butterflies waited—the train carried the flower.

In the arching cavern of the train station, they came for her. They were three; contemporary viceroys, three of the ten: the board who ruled, directed, and guided in the name of the kingdom, the company, and its sovereign, the president. In this great city of the East, they met. They of it, of it she would join.

"It" was one of the largest and most well-known of all the national publishing companies. Respected. Of books, magazines, and newspapers, the dissemination of the printed they were. To all was their mission: to thrive through service, and yes, give of their excesses. From those of wealth to those of poverty, no one, nothing was excluded. From the arts, music, and museums to bread, soup, and shelter came material reflections of good … constantly omnipresent, constantly fulfilled.

Of itself, the company was not lavish but was inwardly generous. Reaching the apogee of its rise was dependent upon those of its work. To them, they exhibited and gave also of their excesses. Proper "business decorum." Not only a place of livelihood, but also a place to live they provided. From the train they took her there: a small one-room flat of efficiency and frugality. Furnished. Only blocks from the publishing house, it was a building of residence to many of this company. Hers, her new home ... fresh paint. Who was here before? How long? What might be the reason for its present emptiness—the stories of this place? Time, the great provider of answers and the provider of solutions for these and other questions, would do both ... time.

The next morning, her first day of employment began. The boardroom and the ten. Four other "new ones" were with her. A room imagined as it was similar to ones she saw at the university. A long, dark, and highly-polished table of wood was the centerpiece. Padded leathers chairs surrounded the table with one larger chair at the end. Five opposite five they sat. The president's chair was empty. Away on business of the company. Standing at one end of the table, the five new employees listened. Welcoming with words of encouragement and what their expertise could contribute, the chairman spoke. Brief was his speech, but lengthy in meaning. Finished, shaking hands with the ten, the five departed. The feeling of importance, just as the action of the elevator carrying them, went also—lower. Stopping at five different floors, one by one, they went to their assignments. The last stop. She exited and entered....

Her corner office was one of many that surrounded a large open center area with many desks; their occupants quietly speaking, exchanging words and documents. A humanized corral it was, not with sounds of animals but machines making the incessant, monotonous, and hypnotic noises—typewriters. Fingers silently pushing and pounding, the operators labored with eyes constantly looking from keys to paper—results of efforts .... "Research and

Submissions" with her name was the sign on her small room. A desk. And yes, a typewriter. A wooden cabinet. Also placed on the desk it was as if a lone sentinel, a soldier, upright and black with only one arm hanging, an open mouth, always at attention: a telephone. It did not march, but took orders in cadence through the dial at its base—the most modern of the day. Behind the desk, a bare wall ... the alpha, the diploma would hang. Would there be an omega?

Her office and her title would be her work; the site would be the start or the finish for material to be considered for publication. Because it was written was no assurance that it would be brought to the people. Of sifting, separating, selecting, and seizing things that possessed promise and merit, she would excel.

Over the next year, her work became something more than simply selecting material to be considered for publication; things that possessed merit—potential. More positive responses came from readers, not of what she had written, but of that which she scrutinized, made corrections for improvement, and made more appealing. Her name was not known outside this company, but inside ... those on the floors above took notice. Even to the top. The president.

On a Friday in February of her second year, she was invited—she felt "summoned" to his office. Entering the elevator, the accordion lattice door of brass was closed by its attendant. Whirring and clanking, it lifted them upward. To his office was a walk past other rooms of stately appearance to a large one with an imposing door of walnut; "President" in plain bold letters, with his name in smaller letters below. It was the office of highest significance, and the occupied one of longevity—or brevity. With his secretary accompanying, she entered his office: simple in furnishings but formal in feeling. Clasping her hand, smiling, he welcomed her.

The president. Three times her age. Zero to infinity of all in this place. His stature was imposing, almost grandeur in sight; a three-piece suit with its lapel adorned with a rose. Always. His presence and voice were evident; when he spoke it was not "to" or "at" but rather oratorical, almost ceremonial, and if negativity were needed, it was disguised with softness. Everyone understood. These were only small elements of the almost reverence he was given by those he commanded. Yet there was something about this man: whispered history of this modern centurion.... He was once a promising writer of intellectual talent, at the precipice of literary greatness. But an event had occurred, the knowledge and omission of which the people did not have that would clarify and explain. They knew the before and after, but just as the ellipsis in literature, something was left out, left to the imagination of the reader. The ellipsis "...": these three dots, simple punctuation ... the unknown. The time and events symbolized by them were not known or could be recounted. Suppositions and mystery were constant and rife. Tragedy was the consensus, but not the physical. An enigma, a secret kept, covered and suppressed. Forever?

As an organizer and leader, disciplined in his ways of fairness and honesty to all, he delegated and directed this company. This legion, this small army of soldiers followed and labored to continuous success not through a venture of daily work, but an almost adventure of their lives. Love. Passion. Desire. The triumvirate of his profession. The reasons he existed in his position. Deserved greatness and fame would be his as its leader and not as an author; he would write no more.

Thanking her and complimenting her on her current work, they walked to his desk; sitting opposite, he placed his hand on a stack of papers, a thick stack, neatly arranged, a manuscript. It looked like so many of those she had reviewed for acceptance or rejection. As he lifted it and turned it toward her, she held her thoughts and voice. It was hers, her manuscript, her potential. The book to be, her novel, was a distant and long ago hope of dreams; but in reality, she knew of its chances. So many others as she, the fate of the first attempt they suffered; dashed expectations from rejection. She was prepared....

Composed over four years at the university, its construction was formed from the education of that place; the many courses of study, especially those of her professor, the professor emeritus. Constantly changing, constantly improving, and constantly persevering, she wrote. Always disguised and concealed from the world, the ongoing book was never alone ... nourishment and protection until its full maturity was reached with satisfaction ... the last chapter, the last word.

The president and the professor emeritus. Associated for many years, these two frequently sought advice, exchanged ideas, and delved deeply into their mutual philosophies of their individual work and position. The educator had told the publisher of her, his former student, an individual whom he considered of the highest aptitude, and expertise in capabilities who could contribute, who could thrive and give. She also possessed something greater—a gift. A writer. An author. That gift was borne out in the book, the book she had written, the book she had left behind. She wanted her professor to examine, appraise, and judge its entirety; of merit or not. Yes, he did that and would share with whomever he desired as she agreed. Powerfully connected, the book and diploma, even apart for the passed years, now together.

He looked at her, smiled, and asked if she could give some history of her book. She related much of what he already knew; of her studies and how they paralleled the book, how she attempted to connect words with senses, feelings, and surroundings, keeping the reader engaged, using the mysterious glue—the bond of one's mind—to bring the story closer, include another character: the reader.

Yes, he told her, this book did just as she described. Continuing, he said it was of proper and exact construction; it flowed; was ingenious, inspiring, graceful with imagination and drama. Then the ultimate. It was worthy of publication ... more than something of possibility, something epic, as only very few accomplished; a classic work of enjoyment, contemplation, and education. Both now smiling, he told her it had been accepted, without reservations and bypassing her department! But she must still continue working; she could prepare the legal documents required between author and publisher. Her thoughts were a galaxy of wonderment as she left his office, yet feeling humility throughout her being.

Nine months passed quickly. November. Tomorrow. Publication. The end of anticipation. Many came by her office—offering flowers, cards, and verbal congratulations, the usual starter for a book launch. Just before noon, a copy boy stopped and told her their president wanted to see her in his office. The top floor. Entering the elevator, her thoughts were of sunshine and rainbows ... no clouds.

Offering his hand, he greeted her again. Praise. Congratulations. As he had told her before, her novel was a work that soared beyond expectations of the loftiest imaginations; comparable to, if not above, the authors of past and present, those of notoriety and fame. A copy of her book was on his desk, opened, under the illumination of his reading lamp. They sat. He began to speak, reading a passage from her book. This paragraph, he said, was a description that evoked powerful feelings, not only of the book's characters but of the reader also. These words entwined the reader into an emotional and personal participation in the fabric of the story. It was not the most important but was the link: that which made the connection from writer to reader, to create one more character, albeit one of physical disconnect—the one holding, reading....

He then opened another book and began to read again. Her facial expression, her thoughts: where was this change to another book leading? After only a few sentences, she instantly knew. She had inserted another's words into her thoughts. Now in her book. The most grievous of sins in literature it was. Plagiarism. Yes, she remembered, she told him. She had done this, but that passage, that paragraph had been given reference and credit by her, with quotation marks, the antivenom of the deathly poison of plagiarism. But, in this, in her great work, they were absent. She knew that he was the last, if need be, the ultimate editor of everything that was published to the world from this company, especially one of this possibility.... She knew he was the great appraiser and approver, beyond the penultimate, the senior editor. The last one to see. The last one to approve. The usual. But not of this book. Had the senior editor been questioned? Impossible as she had departed suddenly for "personal matters" and could not be reached. Twelve hundred miles to the west.

Her thoughts vaulted past the personal. She was aware that competition among publishers was past fierce, and to some, more than just for a single book, ready to reduce, to send its opponent's very life into the permanent exile of bankruptcy. And just blocks away it resided: the most antagonistic and biggest rival. It would take them only a short time to read her book and to find it: this "stolen" passage. To several newspapers of sensation, this "revelation," this discovery, would be sent. The vipers of publicity, who consumed only the needed truth, with innuendos and the subtle ways of a pickpocket, would turn a temporary literary illness into an epidemic of malignant aversion against any "offender."

Preservation of professional and human integrity was the foremost of reasons for immediate reaction to this crisis. Next came the basic and worldly: the prevention of economic strangulation from man's greed. Protection through destruction was the answer. The books, all twenty-five thousand of the first printing, were already being burned in the furnaces next to the pressroom. "Printing and binding problems" were the reasons given. Partial truth, but the truth.... After corrections, publication would be "rescheduled." Similar occurrences had happened in the past, but this one had something more: magnitude, mortal magnitude.

He told her that only two, and possibly three, knew and would ever know the true reasons for these events: the two of them and, with question, the senior editor. Mistakes can be corrected, he told her. He could only judge and decide what was before him. Hesitating and looking away, he also said, softly, that if one had committed a sin, it could be forgiven. Hers or the senior editor's, she wondered. He knew the impact of his words and he knew that if he had looked into her eyes, the one word "sin" would have been accusatory. His belief, faith, and trust in so much had been wounded—not destroyed, but challenged by what was known. When and if the unknown could be unraveled, there might be resolution or restitution or.... He told her she would not be dismissed, "fired," a word in the common vernacular that was more than detestable to him. Her office and belongings would be the same, but her position, her work, would be changed. Publishing purgatory. There to remain until....

His final words to her were of the rose he wore. It was a "complex" flower. But it possessed the antithesis of the complex issues they now faced: it was the symbol of balance, hope, promise, and "new beginnings." It would remind him of those things and this day. He would continue, not "to find a way out" but a way of "new beginnings." Would time, patience, and diligence provide the answers?

Immediate was her despair, born in the land of desolation, giving way to desperation. It would be ever-present, but kept at survivor's distance with her sword of hope, sharpened by the words of the rose. Her career, now in dangerous question, she unsheathed that sword.... The first and last tears of the day were dried. At this moment, from the present to the future continuous, her personal being would act: "I am composing myself" to *I will be re-composing myself.*" For all that was and all that is to come, those elements she possessed would be realigned, restored to continue, but with detours—of the mind, body, spirit, and those who would support and sustain ... perpetual they would be.

Simultaneous with the meeting of these two, an internal bulletin had been sent throughout the company. Word passed. Their project would be rescheduled due to known reasons. Human reaction, on all of the floors of that building, discussions, "talk," was happening.

Some whispered, some used logic, but there was a dampness, a loss of spirit that pervaded on that day.

She returned. They were waiting. Her floor. Solace, comfort, and assurance. Words. They were repelled from an inward and dark place, but outward, accepted with a gentle smile and thank yous. On her life's highest and lowest days, she left that place, that company, those people. Today passed and, lost with it, was hope. Tomorrow. Without publication, she would return.

The remaining days, the weeks of November and December, were less in their light, but within that building became longer in work. Controlled chaos at times. Numbers. Deadlines. Temporary frustrations.... But she, focused, efficient, and prepared, always seemed to be waiting for the next batch to be placed on her desk. With mental and mechanical monotony, her performance and production were incentives to some, but impediments to others. Outwardly, she and her office kept the gates of operation open, but inward, the lava of life had cooled, slowed almost to petrification. She thought of those in other offices, the ones above....

Two weeks before Christmas at her office he stopped, pushing his cart of waste. Ethan. A custodian. A janitor. They knew of each other, only in passing, not in the personal. He knew of her, of what was known of her book, of its sudden paralysis. Of the immediate, he knew that the Christmas Eve company party was coming; that they were afternoon affairs. These ended as night came, allowing all to be in their homes for their own special times. Human, heartfelt concern he had, as he imagined that she would be alone on that night. His thoughts were correct. He would act.

He began by telling her that her work kept him quite busy, almost like a racehorse he felt. Both laughing, he spoke of the upcoming company party. Yes, she was coming, but only for a short time. He then said if she had no commitments after, it would please him if she would join his wife and him for a simple dinner. Not wanting to go, but not wanting to disappoint, she accepted. Thanking him, it would be "just dinner" and no gifts. Agreeing, a quick handshake and smile, they parted.

December 24th came. The afternoon annual celebration, one on each floor, was held in their building. Too many people; there were no rooms large enough to accommodate all. As the day ended, and darkness began, the festivities closed also. She and Ethan left into the cold of that night. They walked on that snowy Christmas Eve, down the brightly lit street, past the stores with windows filled with their holiday fare, people with muffled chatter carrying their harvest of their seasonal work—presents. Before crossing a main street, they waited for a street car to pass, with sparks from its wheels of steel showering and quickly falling, their bright and brilliant lives quickly extinguished in the snow. A fleeting thought she had, a personal requiem: those sparks and her life—much, so much the same. Rounding a corner, down a smaller and darker street they went, not ominous and foreboding, but different.

They went into his house, his home: a small basement dwelling under the first of many row houses. Inside, almost in a corner, a small iron stove, with a bucket of coal as its attendant, complemented an atmosphere more than the warmth of survival it created. A small sofa and two chairs further provided, in their arrangement, a sense of human closeness and security. Across the room in the center of the largest wall it was: a small table covered with a faded cloth of red and green—these days, this season. At one end of the table, a radio, with a cloudy and dimly lit dial, played. Christmas carols came from it with the intermittent crackling of unwanted accompaniment—static. In the center was a Christmas tree, almost a foot in its height. A tree that was not of the forest but of an oven—the kiln of a potter. This object was once an exquisite ceramic creation, adorned only with tiny angelic figurines ... earth and Heaven, joined. Yet time, the years, had begun to win the struggle of its existence; giving way to spots of the red clay from which it was made. On one side of this tree was a small manger scene, cut from perhaps a magazine or a card, modern in its physical depiction but Biblical in its eloquence. On the opposite side of the tree were three wrapped presents across from the Three Wise Men ... three who carried gifts ... three then, three now. Three gifts, not from men long ago on this Night of Nights, not from mortals to the Immortal, but from one mortal one to another they were. Not rare and precious but common, yet they could be used in infinite fashion, limited only by the mind of man. Their time would come....

From a small adjoining room, the kitchen, she entered: Ethan's wife. Arms extended, open wide with a smile, she embraced their guest. This woman, obvious in her genteel manners, became instantly an affectionate and benevolent addiction to their visitor. This introduction, the meeting of these in this place with subdued suddenness, did not overwhelm, but gave an immediate sense with aura of another world, another time—something else, something beyond its simplicity and meager surroundings existed. She felt it. Before this earthly and Holy evening ended, it would be firmly fixed, this peaceful and comforting unknown to all.

Around a small round table they sat. Just enough room. The kitchen. The light that softly lit was not of a crystal chandelier such as those in homes across that town but from a single flame, a candle.

The aroma of that to be consumed was as sensory music, a culinary waltz in waiting. From the fork to the palate, this dance would begin. Few in its contents, but regal in effect it was: a casserole—the light and dark of the fowl, peas of green, orange carrots, cranberries, and rice, not of the gaudy or glamorous but of generosity. A Christmas casserole of celebration, cheer, comfort, and caring.

The crescendo, the culmination, was the dessert made of apples, flakes of oats, raisins, and nuts bathed in a syrup of cinnamon and sugar. All of this was between the layers of a simple hot water crust, "blind baked," irregular in its contours: the signature of a homemade pie. Thick white cream was the velvet cover, not to contain, but to enrich what was to be savored. The satisfaction of the physical, the hunger, was sealed with coffee, all feeling that this basement feast could carry them into the new year. And with that food, the conversations among the three, of families, and Christmases past, happiness surrounded it all. Obvious was the gaiety, its effect and need. On that night, this was only the beginning....

They sat, Ethan, his wife, and guest—she in a chair, they on the sofa. The radio, now strangely without static, played "Angels, From the Realms of Glory." Ethan rose, went to the table, picked up the three presents, and gave them one by one to her, their visitor, their guest, their new friend. For her, in embarrassment, was a flushed face, and tears. But there were to be no gifts? They had agreed when the invitation was offered and accepted. Ethan smiled; his wife, a tear also.

The first opened, thick and weighty, contained a sheaf, a stack of paper; the writing size eight by ten. On the first sheet she noticed a spot and one typed word, and more like this as she shuffled more pages. Not new, but used, used slightly and quickly, by those in their building. Discarded they were in the rush of daily work, by those wanting perfection in their efforts. She knew. These sheets of paper were part of the "process." Ethan in his toils collected these, those with the least of man's imperfections and frustrations, to be saved, to be given one day—this day.

The next gift, a small box. Barely visible on one corner was a tiny black smudge. A bottle of ink. Ebony. The darkest of all colors. The waste, the unused, the overflow from the pressroom was its origin. The last, the most colorful, almost too beautiful to unwrap, was carefully and gently opened: a pen, a fountain pen. Shining, almost glowing in hue and design, it was laid in a bed of soft cotton. She held it, eyes fixed, uncoupled it, and saw the point, diamond in shape with a small hole in its center. An opening not of decoration, but of necessity: air, oxygen, for its gentle and physical pressure, that which pushed and pulled the ink. Just as man did, ironically this instrument needed oxygen as well. Without it, the pen and its blood—ink—would not flow. Inert. Inanimate. At the very end was the polished, tiny tip: the nib of gold. It was the place of translation from the mind to the paper. Here, ink would flow from thoughts to words to be manifested from its holder.

She opened the bottle, dipped the pen into the ink, and slowly pulled the small lever on its side—filling, bringing to life, preparing for the first words to come.

"God's Blessings"

In flowing script she wrote on that first piece of paper. She handed it to Ethan. Looking at it, pausing, he told her that she wrote her name as if it had been written by an angel. Her name? She disguised her inner reaction of collapse without expression. He could not read! Illiterate. Yet she knew from years of education how to encompass a situation that was so very common. Illiteracy was not a disease to be contracted or spread, but an affliction, one that could be overcome. Permanently. She looked, and thanking him, said only his name. And waited. Ethan's wife softly gasped, her hand covering her mouth, and began softly crying. Ethan dropped his head to his knees, looking at the floor, told her that he, they, could neither read nor write. She replied there were many as they, and they were not alone. Verbal diversion was needed.

She asked him if he could count. Yes, to one hundred and no more, he said. Why? Because no more in living was ever needed. Especially in his world, his life, the results of his energy, never reached past the century mark—in dollars. One hundred was more than he would ever need, she said. Twenty-six, she emphatically continued. Reading and writing require only counting to twenty-six, that is all, now and forever: the alphabet. Perplexed, confused, and bewildered, Ethan and his wife looked at each other. Aghast. Ethan walked over, and from a small bookshelf, lifted the one book they possessed: a Bible. And this? Yes, that, that is the most important of all ever written, she said, all of it with only twenty-six letters. He opened the book. A page marker. He said he could not read the passage, but knew it ... John 3:16. It was about Christmas, tonight and tomorrow, His birth and The Great Promise. Ethan recited, "Whosoever believeth in Him will not perish, but have everlasting life." Jesus. Christmas.

After this powerful revelation, the invitation she offered to Ethan and his wife: she would teach them, about letters, about words, how to write and read. Would she, could she do this for them? The honor and privilege would be hers. But first, Ethan asked if she could write something of his, their life, ancestors, and history to give his children who were grown and had moved away. A definite, recorded legacy that many such as he did not have. Yes, together these two would happen: his learning and his written history.

The ending of this Eve neared; Christmas Day would come in one hour. The parting of these three was not a "good-bye," but a "We'll meet again." Ethan's wife remained, doing an enjoyable chore—the dishes. She and Ethan bundled up for the cold night. He would accompany her to the streetcar stop, a ten-minute ride to her flat. Waiting for the car, Ethan revealed one last thing: his wife, long ago in childhood, had suffered an accident, the result being damage to her sight, leaving her partially blind. Reading and writing could never be. But she had lived, functioning well in all other aspects of life. His wife considered this a diversion, not a handicap. With Ethan's ability to read, their burdens would be made lighter. A "Merry Christmas" was exchanged as she climbed into the streetcar.

The new year came and they began ... the letters, the alphabet, writing and reading. She was amazed at Ethan's progress, his learning from the elementary to the advanced. Just as profound was his history, its retention, and the recall in the most minute of details. His mind, his memory was encyclopedic, indexed not only with facts, but also with thoughts, opinions, and feelings. Those days for both were not of drudgery that many endured, but days of delight—as picnics. And always, they started with food for the occasion; here, homemade biscuits and jelly crafted from her hands, Ethan's wife.

What had begun as only a wish that written history be fashioned to be passed to Ethan's relatives became a project that grew and matured as his skills did. A parallel would form. She would become his university, his professor emeritus. Traveling this upward path helped her wound to heal, but still present there existed mental scars.

From the early days came the early chapters, elementary in construction and information. As she taught, he advanced throughout as noticed in the complexities of all chapters, to the last of twenty-six— all he, anyone, ever needed.... Combining all the letters and making words, time yielded, through their concentration and dedication, a realization. More, much more than a calendar of one's life, it became a journal of living replete with history and life lessons intensified throughout, by reason, and by its innate virtue—learning.

Of the pen, ink, and the paper given on that Christmas Eve and the Spirit surrounding them combined to create something even greater. A manuscript. It would become a book, *Ethan's Journey* the title. Distantly similar to her diploma, it not only signified but revealed the same—a passage....

Time... two more years. Another ending of the calendar. Another Christmas Eve day. And another traditional holiday celebration. But this year there was a difference: location. Not in the usual, not on any of the many floors where those people of perception sought perfection, but the lowest at times, the place of destruction, under the earth's surface: the basement. The pressroom. Loading docks for trucks. The furnaces. The "reason": "malfunction and repair" of those furnaces. There was no heat in that building except for in this lowly place. The smell of it: machines, oil, and smoldering coal were replaced by the aroma, the fragrance of spruce, pine, and fir—the trimmed branches of trees on the dark floors above, burning slowly in the furnaces. Warmth for this place, this day.

This large area had been cleared, cleaned, and rearranged, transforming it into a festive hall. Lights of all colors strung from the great beams above, and ribbons, garlands, and candles created a surrounding that brought forth personal sensations to each one present. Many round tables were covered with cloths of white linen; a bowl of punch, cups, cookies, and sweets in the center of each one. Eight chairs around. A wrapped present in each one. In the front, a raised platform was arranged with a podium in the center. On each side of the lectern was a single chair; a setting for the traditional Christmas message from the president. The entirety of all was this place, this change of venue on this day ... something as a zephyr of quizzical gaiety was present as this place filled ... something.

She had arrived and, surprised as everyone, would be kept longer than planned by her expectations being overwhelmed. Ethan, already there, sat with others of the custodial staff. She greeted him, all at his table, and walked to her seat nearby with her prior thoughts of it being the last of them she would attend, as her place there had long since reached stagnation. But now, this mental process was substituted by the totality of the unexpected. Two basements of different times, of different events, but on the same day—two years apart.

Outside, as darkness approached, inside the end of the commemoration would become a magnification of the first Christmas and that of this day. From the president it came.... The darkest of green was his suit, contrasting in its lapel was red of the rose, not one, but two small ones, side by side. As he stood, the audience became silent, still. He greeted them with words of the season, the past year, and the coming of the New Year. He then held up a book, the Bible, and continuing he spoke:

Men of long ago wrote, just as is done here. They wrote of the earth, how it began, and how it will end. And they wrote of man, how he was created ... his many triumphs and failures. Of all that was and that which will come to humankind was written by mortals but composed in the Heavens, by Him, the Decision Maker, the Final Editor, the one of grace and forgiveness, our Lord, the one God. All that was foretold happened and continued. A birth that gave hope, from One who was promised by the Father that all who followed Him would continue beyond earthly mortality to live forever.... And today, here, we celebrate that miracle of long ago, and as was then, this day, may it also be one of new beginnings.

Pausing, he looked over his people, then requested that she and Ethan come forward. Heads turned, eyes fixed, questions thought, with only the sounds of the footsteps of those two, those sitting watched the two walking. Arriving and standing on either side of him, the president removed the roses from his lapel and passed one to her, this worker, this writer, and one to Ethan, this custodian, this laborer—both who had endured and persevered....

Putting aside the Bible, he held high two books, one in each hand. With covers and letters so bold and bright, they could be seen from the front to the rear of that vast room: one her book, her novel, and the other *Ethan's Journey*: two books, two lives. He began to tell the stories of the past years, of how these books came to be on this day. Discoveries, only two, would be magnified through time.

The first came from her misfortune and that Christmas Eve dinner, that evening of an unseen Spirit ... this discovery was of Ethan's secret, his being unable to read or write. Time passed and she would give his education, his learning, by transcribing a life retained in his memory through the pen. Without Ethan's knowledge, she took it, as she had done with hers many years ago, not to a professor but to a president. She felt of Ethan's work as those two did of hers—potential. He accepted it, and two weeks later these two met again. He said of this custodian's work that it was unique and powerful, just as hers was, yet in a different way, and equal in possibilities. She heard his words, "just as hers was," and related them to her novel prior to its precipitous downfall. She understood, but also felt a cryptic sensation....

The second discovery was by Ethan. A box, before he could read, not knowing what was written on it, was retrieved by him from a bin of waste that was to be destroyed, burned. It had come from the senior editor's office, the one long since departed ... unknown. Large dark letters, the ones to be noticed, were accompanied by smaller lines of writing on its top. Intuition. Save this. There was a corner in a large storage room where he kept such things. There it stayed ... until. As time passed, his learning progressed—reading. And over the long many months, his secret was kept, but was about to become known. On one of his random visits to that room he remembered the box. He read of its contents. He took it. The top floor.

Custodians never requested to see the president. He knew that Ethan was unaware of his own manuscript being in his possession. Why this thought-provoking request? They met. The president found in that box a treasure of immense meaning and proportions: there on that page of her questioned manuscript, those quotation marks," ", were present. A mistake, not a sin. From Ethan, the president now had the answer to what caused this mystery of devastation. Two books, two lives, separate and alone, on this day would be forever connected. The president would be the one to consecrate this grand joining, and yes, one of new beginnings. In two weeks they would be published, these books, without the history of how they became, but only with what was written within—what they would become.

From the podium was seen a sea of white: handkerchiefs and linen napkins, a surrender not of war, but of emotions. Of hearts they came in silence, liquid feelings: tears. The soul, from its deepest part, was signaling celebration of its conqueror, the Spirit.

From the lost hopes of long ago yesterdays, struck down by the frailty and weakness of man, of the Pen and the Rose it came: a story of redemption, just as Christmas....

The Covenant

BELLS. Of churches, schools, and dining rooms, their crisp and lingering rings, for the beginning of worship, learning, and eating, they called. But there was one that signaled not only a beginning but an ending of constant daily acts: the transaction of labors. This bell was on a door; it rang upon opening and closing, people entering and leaving. It was a place of washing, drying, ironing, and the careful arranging and packaging of many types and sizes of clothes. It was also a place that extended the life of many of these garments: sewing, darning, patching, and blending to restore. It was a cleaning establishment, a laundry. And in those times, no machines existed to ease and streamline these tasks. Here, by hand, all was accomplished. Only four hands: a widower and his eight-year-old son performed this work. The wife, a mother and companion, had been lost as were many to a common and prevalent disease. There were no medicines to cure, only prayers against this pestilence—pleurisy.

On the first day of the month, it rang, this doorbell, and as on every one of these days the landlord came to collect the rent. He was the owner of this building on the corner of a busy city street. He lived above the only business in that building, the laundry. Not dilapidated, but "run-down" it was, with three "For Rent" signs in the other vacant spaces. Less than minimal was his care and upkeep of this structure, but maximum he was in his greed, a fact known to all. He reminded his only tenant that he was late with his last month's payment, although the first day of the past month had been on a Sunday. No excuses. Rent was due "on or before the first day of each month." His landlord also reminded him that he was receiving more than that for which he paid. Not only a place of business, but their home. The man and his boy lived in a back section with a "front door" opening into an alley. "Kindness" from the mind of avarice, he allowed, he "gave" them a place to live—"free."

Saturdays, closing at noon, the two continued their labors. But on these days, the tasks were a mile away. The orphanage. They loaded their wagon with what was needed: washboards, soap, brushes, needles, threads, and buttons. The children always met them with squeals, laughter, and hugs, for these chores had been transformed into playful games. And always, these two who gave through their work, were paid at the end of the day: a bowl of steaming, fresh potato soup with rolls hot from the oven.

This man and his son also gave to others of their "spare" time. Of the streets, the vagrants and homeless had needs just as those of means. They ate a meager meal in the backroom while their worn clothes were washed and cleaned with the same care and concern; they were never considered any less than those whose clothes hung to dry adjacent to their tattered ones. The policeman, who daily walked this street, a visible protection, never asked, but was always told his blue tunic was becoming "a bit dusty." He graciously accepted this trade—this exchange of human energy. Even to the unknown and unwanted the laundryman and his son were called: those who were taken to their final place in potter's field, though they had come from poverty and more, they were dressed as if going to a celebration—in a plain wooden box.

One day, a stranger, not the usual customer—not the factory worker, the baker, the fishmonger, or those others who worked and lived nearby—came into the laundry. Dressed in a suit and carrying a bag, he walked to the counter of business. He introduced himself only as "Paul." He said he was an aide, a secretary for a man. These were his superior's clothes in the bag. Smiling and opening it, he placed its contents on the counter: three white shirts and a fine tailored suit of beige linen lined with silk. Paul said he had been informed that the man and his son performed very special things with clothes. Picking up one of the shirts, the laundryman replied that they prided themselves on their work—and one of their specialties was "shirts and collars." Terms were agreed upon; the clothes would be finished and collected in three days.

First, the pockets of the clothes were always examined for forgotten items. In the pants pockets of this linen suit four pennies had been left. He placed these in a cup, on a shelf with other cups, and on a small piece of paper wrote the name of the owner. He would set these aside and always return them. Yet, there were others in his profession who acted differently with these forgotten items, these things that had been left behind. They would keep them for themselves: a one-way journey. And sometimes when asked by their patrons, they might return a portion. This "gesture" gave the impression of an honest business person. But depending upon what the object might be, its value, the reply might be that nothing had been found, keeping all that was left and forgotten by another. Their justification was the sign, "Not responsible for items left in clothes." But in this place, as in the lives of these two, reigned the principle of return. Giving back, not taking.

Three days later, three shirts, one suit, and four pennies he gave to Paul, telling him the coins had been found in the pants pockets. A thank you and money for work performed were exchanged. Saying no more, Paul left, the bell sounding his departure.

One week passed and he returned. And again, Paul presented three white shirts and another linen suit. Baltic blue was its color. Three days again? Of course, plenty of time. Not thinking, he began the process: the same cursory look at the shirts, then the search of the suit—nothing. One last place searched was the small watch pocket in the coat. Squeezing a finger into its small opening, he felt two coins: more pennies. But when he pulled them out, they were not copper but gold—two Half Eagles, a tender of those times, ten dollars the total of the two. Surprised, he thought the man or Paul had been rushed, didn't have the time for thoroughness—it was a small, almost hidden, pocket. The gold coins, into a cup; the name, Paul. This routine and exercise continued, from pennies to gold to scraps of paper, from the insignificant to the valuable—all were set aside and returned.

As the weeks passed, Paul would come, bringing the same: three shirts and a suit. And periodically nothing was left, nothing was found. But, always, when it did occur, always true to form—it was given back. One day, it would be the last time that something was found hidden in the garments, something in one of those pockets. This time, it was in the breast pocket of the coat: a compact Bible, with something as a bookmark, between two of its pages. Opening it, he found two five dollar bills folded at the passage of the Ten Commandments. This would be the last thing to be left behind— retrieved and returned. These two men had spoken of all things that had been left by this unknown man whom Paul represented. Absentmindedness? Perhaps it seemed so, but Paul said this man always knew—and remembered.

Taking the shirts and the suit, the laundryman began the task of washing and finishing. All that remained was the ironing of the shirts with special attention to the collars. The irons were heated on the hot stove top; next, he worked with calculated movement, careful not to leave creases or wrinkles. Starch, mixed with water, was sprinkled to give smoothness and body not only on the surface, but throughout. As he was ironing the last shirt, the bell rang. He looked up momentarily and a sizzling sound came from the iron. The smell. The shirt had been scorched. Burned. He had learned how, through past experience, to remedy such accidents. More starch. Less heat. He did this and it disappeared, but below this place another brown spot appeared. Continuing, he moved the iron in a different direction. He was concerned—his efforts were failing although this usual method had always succeeded before. He stopped and looked: now the shape was an "x" about one inch in dimension. One last attempt: thicker starch and gentle heat. Lifting, placing, and moving the iron slowly,

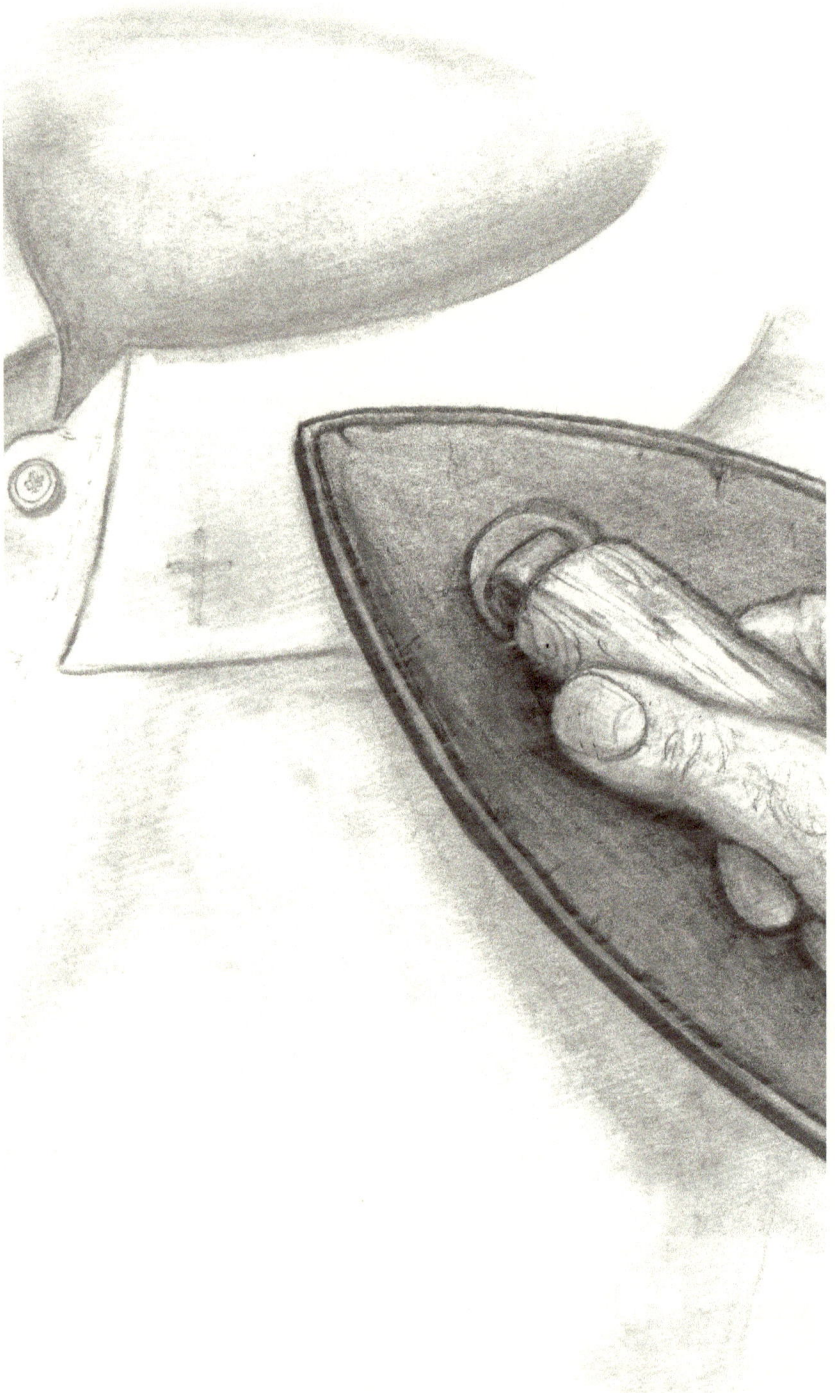

the scorch disappeared! In disbelief, he stared. He moved the shirt and its collar in different directions. Still doubting, he took the shirt outside, into the bright sunlight.

Then he saw it: not the remnants of the brown "x" but a cross, whiter than the rest of the shirt material. A cross, in the same shape as the one on the church spire across the street. He went back inside with the shirt. The door closed behind him, the bell ringing a bit louder and longer. The collar on the shirt appeared as the others—no evidence— only smooth and white. Inside his eyes did not see it, but he touched it. He could feel it. That which had happened, in its entirety, would be told, and the good and honest thing he did, the restitution.

This accident and the subsequent occurrence he told to Paul upon his return. Although on the surface, all had been restored; below it was the truth. Nothing would be withheld. He took Paul outside into the sunshine, then into the light of the laundry: Paul saw it in both lights. He handed Paul an envelope. In it were the past day's profits. Five dollars. Five times what a shirt of the day cost. His insistence was that the repaired shirt and money for a new one were to be accepted. It was not only a replacement, but a restitution and affirmation of the core, the very center and essence of his life; it was the Spirit of his heart.

Paul said only thank you and left. He continued to return, but nothing else was ever left, ever forgotten in the clothes he would bring. And the collar—knowledge remained, but never would be mentioned again ... ever.

Summer came, and with it, clothes of the season arrived at his business, greater in variety and amount, creating more hours of work. He had a bit more money, and always a portion, a tithe, would go into a special envelope. That amount increased also. And on one of these scorching days when Paul was present, a change came that would bring an upheaval, more mental than physical, for this laundryman, and for his life.

A loud pop and a bang they heard coming from the street: the noise of the newest and most improved of motorized inventions, a truck that had stopped. The noise was a backfire. When the engine was turned off, it made a sound as if it were a mechanical horse not wanting to halt. Two more trucks arrived. More backfires. Suddenly, the landlord appeared with the men from the truck, pointing inside where the two stood looking out. Eviction! The immediate cataclysmic thought. The outsiders disappeared around the corner of the building. Saying nothing, paying for the clothes, Paul left.

For the remainder of that day, with noises from above, men carried goods, boxes, and furniture down the outside stairs, loading and stacking them into the trucks. The laundryman continued his daily tasks, sure that the owner would appear with it—the notice. Anxiety, proceeding to almost the point of panic, lessened with the ending of the day and the absence of this old—or new—owner. When would this person return?

The next morning more trucks appeared. Had they come to remove him, his business, his life? Two men entered, one carrying several papers. The judgment? The first paper was handed to him, and at the top in bold letters were the words "Work Orders." The building was to be repaired, painted, and remodeled, they told him. This would ultimately mean one thing: his rent would be dramatically increased. He would not be evicted, but economically forced out. He was taken by surprise when they asked what color paint he preferred. And would his business be interrupted if they could also replace the damaged wood around the front window? Temporarily relaxed, he said no and selected a paint color from the samples that were shown to him.

In early September, it was finished in outward appearance and structure within. It became a place displaying a welcoming strength from its renewal. Passersby noticed. Business increased even more. Improvement came, not only because of changes in his new surroundings, but also from the consistency of his work for others, through his labors. Why? Because he was not tempted by these new advantages as many others might have been, leading to self-aggrandizement. His prosperity was the result of charging fair fees for his work, of doing his best for everyone, encircled by his indefatigable honesty.

Two more months passed. December. And each day, many times, the bell would ring. And with each ringing, his inner bell of repressed despair also rang. Would it be the old or the new owner, the landlord? No one came for the rent. The weather, with cold and snow, came, and thick coats, sweaters, and garments of warmth came to him. On one of the early days of the month, he returned— Paul. But not alone.

A man taller than Paul came with him, carrying a leather case, dressed in a wool overcoat covering an impeccable suit. Was this the new owner? Was this Paul's superior, for whom he carried out orders? Would this be the day he would wash no more? This man was introduced, his name and title known throughout the city: he was the founder of the most prestigious of all the legal firms. A lawyer, an attorney for matters of legality, of the living and of those who once lived.

The lawyer opened his case and withdrew several papers. Handing them across the counter, he asked the laundryman to read them. Having left his glasses in the back washroom, and drying the soapy water from his hands, he apologized and asked if the attorney could please read them.

Be it known. With this statement the lawyer began with a description of the building, its geographic location, its contents, and the land upon which it stood. Legalese was its wording; sometimes more complicated than necessary to prevent frivolous challenges. His last words were a declaration: *With all the aforementioned, it is hereby decreed and duly registered, for the sum of ten thousand dollars, fully negotiated, satisfied, and paid without any future monetary and other impediments, all described and with all rights and privileges, ownership is hereby transferred to....*

Still drying his hands, thoughts of "without further impediments" flashed and raced through his mind. The new owner. The coup de grâce of his business, his future. But then the unexpected, benevolent shock when he heard it: the name— it was his! Staring at Paul and the attorney, his intensity of interest was confounded but controlled as he listened and the reading continued.

From this day forward and the future beyond, all that is and will ever be known to you and everyone is contained within this document. With only two caveats by which you will abide, you will forever possess. The first, there are to be no inquisitions of its origins or reasons. The second, you shall maintain the continuance of your life as it has been lived.

The three all knew, all realized the significance beyond the business substance and all also knew that further words beyond their just concluded meeting did not exist. All were quiet as the documents were signed and witnessed, and then placed in the leather case. And with this ending, the clouds of doubt were vanquished into oblivion. As the door opened and the two were leaving, turning and smiling, Paul said softly, "Merry Christmas." The door closed; the bell rang. Paul would never return.

It did arrive and pass as it had for two thousand years, Christmas, and forever would return until....

The following summer, in July, he was returning from the newsstand retrieving the old, unsold papers he used in his work, given in exchange for the cleaning of the newsman's aprons. Then he saw it on the front page of an international paper, several months old as they were transported by steamship across the ocean. A picture. The caption read "Il Papa e l'Uomo del Mistero." He returned to the newsstand and asked the newsman what the words said, as this man was of Italian descent and would certainly know: "The Pope and the Man of Mystery." The photograph showed the Pope, bending, about to kiss the right hand of this mystery man, whose head was turned, his face unseen. But the man seemed to be preventing this, as his left hand was lifting the Pope under one arm ... bidding him no, bidding him to rise.

Opening the door of the laundry, he placed the papers on the counter. The picture. Curiosity. He looked at it again, something from within, telling him.... He took it outside, into the bright summer sun, and there on the collar of this man's shirt, it was: the tiny cross. Exhilarated, inspired by this image, he took it back into the building: invisible, just the white, the evenness of it, that collar. Once again, back outside, the same occurrence, the tiny cross. His human, his physical feeling was supplanted by an exultation from the Spirit. His heart and soul entwined, declaring and confirming the second caveat of the covenant, "the continuance of his life as it had been lived." And as He of long ago did, so this man of soap and water, this laundryman, also did: LIVED, just as another Paul once implored everyone to do, with:

Whatsoever things are true
Whatsoever things are honest
Whatsoever things are just
Whatsoever things are pure
Whatsoever things are of good report....

Of Rails and Envelopes

THE GREAT DEPRESSION. In conditions of the times and their effects the world existed; years of economic malfunction from a decrease in industrial production to personal abject poverty—the entire range of it all. In the East some say it started, with the crash of the stock market. But the time of its beginnings was in the South. A "run" on the banks. People withdrawing money. Cash. Yet, the operation of the financial houses was the old-fashioned way because it had always worked: receiving deposits, loaning to borrowers, and timely repayment with interest kept the vaults open and the banks solvent. And a profit. Mathematics in the simplest form revealed if more was withdrawn, loaned, and questionably invested than was deposited and repaid, then failure resulted—cessation of operations.

Closure. No laws of deposit protection existed. The backing of the federal government was never considered or needed—yet.

Accounting and business acumen with an extroversion of confident skills to all gave and sustained the success of his profession. He was a banker. But he as a person and his bank possessed no immunity to the insidious local disease of financial gridlock. The epidemic progressed to a pandemic. One after another, as trees felled by an avalanche, the doors locked, windows shuttered and covered, these pillars of commerce, finance, and personal resources crumbled. By example, he, as well as other employees, were customers of this bank. They saved, borrowed, and had mortgages too. And he suffered as he legally caused—foreclosure. Along with other bankers a public pariah to those whose savings vanished he was. There were a few who knew his fate was the same as theirs, but care and concern they never exhibited.

Westward to his wife's family farm he sent her and his two children. Her parents were there; of Irish descent—the land of a past depression: the great potato famine—they were prepared— *d'ullmhaigh iad*. He would go to the North using his experience, to seek opportunity of stability, to earn and recover that which was lost. In time his plans were to bring them back, to reunite and begin life again....

Seven hundred miles. Late October. A bus would take him to the large metropolis. A once fellow friend was there, a comrade who had worked with him at the same small bank. He had made this journey some years before, seeking and finding greater wealth. This friend was now an executive in conglomeration of a complicated bank that needed many people in its far-reaching operations. A promise was made between the two of them: if either was in need the other one would respond—telegrams were exchanged. The one of living would keep their promise—aid the other—of desperation.

With stops along the journey for rest, food, exchange of passengers, and a relief driver, he rode; his seat on this "express" was also his temporary bed. Two days of monotony he traveled through towns and villages, broken by unspoiled landscapes of fields, farms, and forests—trees. He saw more colors within the leaves than could ever be contained on the palette of a great artist. Seeing these, he remembered science had taught him why they change colors. The green of the spring and summer, was the food for the growth and life of the tree. This being made from the sunlight changed to nourishment, unseen, for its life, was used and stored. As the seasons changed, there was insufficient sunlight to continue the process. An occurrence, marvelous, magnificent, and miraculous took place— "a botanical hibernation." Enough nourishment sufficient for life of this creation was made, stored, and secured for its winter ... the darkness and cold of days to come. This process ended when the colorful leaves fell, and their places on the branches were sealed— the places of the buds of spring time ... life renewed.

As the forests became fewer and the city came closer, his thoughts still were of those trees—and his life. He had lived in the sunlight and had grown. But the days were becoming shorter and darker for him. Was there enough stored to survive? Had his leaves fallen too soon? Had his branches been sealed? Would the green be found in the city? It was not a predicament, it was peril....

Arriving at the bus terminal just after mid-day, he inquired as to the location of his friend's bank. Only six blocks away. Carrying his small suitcase, he walked. He was surprised to encounter so many individuals like himself, some with various sizes and types of baggage—all walking. Also lines of people, some static, others shuffling—moving to where? Finally, he arrived at the bank building. There were no waiting lines. First, he saw a bank guard—always present at these great sites of finance. The sign. He gasped as he read it: "CLOSED UNTIL FURTHER NOTICE." A broken window. He knew. Even the largest, the strongest could not escape and avoid or fight the spread of the affliction. The guard told him it happened two days before; all were gone except the president, and he was preparing to leave this day—as a captain going down with his sinking ship. Or was there a lifeboat waiting? He asked the guard if he knew his friend—yes, he had left the bank and the town the day of the implosion. Nausea. Could the guard inquire inside—anything, any news or instructions left by his friend? Unlocking the door, the guard went inside, closed, and locked the door behind him. Five minutes later he returned with a telegram—returned undeliverable. He opened it and read the words: "Total collapse. Forced to leave. Will try to communicate. So sorry. Good luck." It was not only an envelope containing a message, but a bludgeon that weakened him to near collapse.

The times shattered the promise—not the friend. He had to sit. He had to think. His plan of recovery had abruptly ended. He saw in the fading sunlight of that late afternoon across the street a small park with benches—he went and found an empty one. He read the telegram again—the same effect but now unwritten, the feeling of vulnerability it carried. Another man came and sat at the other end of this bench. Unshaven, dressed in worn and crumpled clothes, he carried a cloth bag over his shoulder. Irregular in its shape, there was a clatter when he placed it on the ground. The neck of a green bottle stuck out of the tightly tied top—wine. His eyes and voice reflected the wine's work as he spoke, but with normal and sincere questions of those in similar circumstances: who was he, what was he, where would he go, and what would he do? Unknown was the banker's answer to the last two questions. The banker asked the same questions: a contractor, a builder was this stranger. As with so many, his business failed almost in the time it took to say "bankrupt," and those who repossessed on orders of his bank came quickly, with an insatiable voracity that bordered on the viciousness of hyenas.

As night was quickly approaching, and it became cooler, the contractor suggested they go to the "yard," a place of relative safety. It would be best to be off the streets—there was an unofficial curfew for everyone's protection. It also reduced the number of those who had themselves arrested for the sole purpose of simply having a place to sleep and a meal—the jail.

The yard was once a place of endings and beginnings of a thriving factory—materials received, goods produced. Connecting this industry to the world were rails that carried trains—it was a rail yard. Upon his arrival, the yard had already begun to fill with men, but a few families could be seen scattered throughout the gathering crowd. It was almost dark and small fires were being built ... warmth, light, and cooking. The two found a place; the contractor gathered some of the many small scraps of wood, and after arranging them neatly in a small square pile, placed a lighted match in the center. The banker was puzzled and asked reasons for the arranging for the burning of the wood, and the placement of the match. The contractor laughed and told him through experience of many nights and many fires that it would burn from the inside to the outside; also burning longer and more evenly made it easier to heat and cook. And it was easier to add to, to keep the fire alive—as long as there was enough energy to feed it from those pieces of wood scattered about that yard.... The banker thought of those forests and the trees and the colored leaves that he had recently seen. Stored energy for life. Were these scraps on this ground the last of that energy for him? Could he find more to keep his fire of life burning?

His thoughts stopped as the contractor rummaged in his bag and withdrew a can of beans. Not speaking, he took his pocket knife and began to cut and open the can. Placing the can in the middle of the fire, pushing in, and arranging the glowing embers closer to it, he said nothing. Both stared at what was before them. As steam began to rise and carry the aroma from those cooking beans, with a spoon, also from his bag, he stirred. Taking two sticks of wood, he lifted the can and placed it between the two of them. He handed the spoon to the banker. The pocket knife carved a narrow piece of wood, which, with an end widened, became the contractor's spoon. The banker, more than surprised, wanted to speak, to ask, and to thank, but was stopped by his companion's raised hand. The contractor said, "I know because I am ... "

The food: beans. Hunger satisfied. The beverage: wine. This combination gave physical nourishment, mental relief, and a temporary euphoria—and a peripheral numbing of the tactile and of the temperature of the night. After an hour, as the fire slowly died, those in the yard leveled themselves to sleep. The contractor signaled, pointing to a place near the overhanging tin roof of the factory. In a corner, a large wooden sign with two sections of iron rails on it, would be their bed. The contractor told him that these people, these temporary overnight residents, never used this place as their energy was not enough to move the pieces of steel. By sliding, and not lifting, the two moved these to the edge of the sign which read, "NO TRESPASSING." The contractor gave the banker a piece of rope: to tie his suitcase to his wrist. "Things" happen here when one is sleeping was the reason for the rope. The wind began to increase and it turned cooler—no, cold. The wine and their long overcoats performed ... sleep.

Noises. He awoke. A man in a blue uniform and hat was shaking him. The police. No. An officer, yes—the Salvation Army. An unexpected storm was rapidly approaching; snow and colder—freezing. As if a lost herd of sheep, these shepherds of care were leading and taking them to their shelter. Sitting up, still in a stupor and confused, the banker looked at the place next to him—the contractor, gone. The rope had been cut but was still tied to his wrist, and his suitcase was nowhere to be seen. This builder, this man only known for hours, was he not a man who projected and seemed sincere, caring, and who shared? Had his human actions of good been a performance that would hide this theft? Had he been one of those "things" that happened during the night? His case contained other clothes, a suit, toiletries, a pair of shoes and socks, in one pair hidden his last $35, the only money he had left.

The shelter. A mile from the yard. Walking with the encouragement of the uniformed ones, this group, some undernourished, some without clothes for the night and cold, all proceeded to a place that would give them another night to see another tomorrow. A very large room, already almost full, was the end of their journey. Given a blanket and shown their place on the hard floor, they stopped, they slept.

Morning. Oatmeal with the many others in that shelter was breakfast. One bowl only. Those who stayed the night were required to leave during the day to seek employment; work for meager hourly jobs to one for a day—more than for wages, something, anything to keep them occupied mentally. He would spend most of that day as he had so many before, as the many others also did—as all living creatures trying to survive. The streets were filled with people—a mix that was a jumbled disorder; from those of seeming direction to those of aimless movement. Lost souls. Occasionally he would stop at businesses and inquire at those without the signs, because there were so many with those signs that read:

"NOT HIRING"
or
"UNEMPLOYED MEN KEEP GOING,
WE CAN'T TAKE CARE OF OUR OWN."

And always he would be told the same: no jobs were available, and apologies, and good luck. Words of courtesy, sincerity, and care they were—human feelings.

Looking across the busy street, something caught not only his eye, but his full attention. His stolen suit was walking in the opposite direction—carrying his suitcase. The banker saw only what was his—not the small man wearing his clothes with the too long pants rolled up. The street, filled with cars and buses, was impossible to cross. He watched. Suddenly a man ran up behind and grabbed the suitcase. It was the contractor! An apparent argument and tug-of-war ensued, won by the contractor. The suit, containing the man, ran and disappeared into the crowd. The banker shouted, the contractor heard and waited a moment before crossing the street with the case. Explaining what had happened while the two slept the night before, the contractor had awoken just after the rope was cut with silence and stealth. He ran after this thief, following him through the night and had finally caught and accosted him as the banker had just witnessed. They opened the suitcase—only shoes. The contractor thought he might know the robber's destination. He would continue to search. These two, meeting less than twenty-four hours before on that bench would meet again.... It was Sunday. He would go to church.

The Sabbath. The day of rest and worship, the church was almost always overflowing. Always open, always warm, and always filled with those who suffered, and some who did not. From the strata of life they came, a site in these times of the only place for past and future reflections. Many, too many looked in the past, never of tomorrow ... hope was a word without meaning. They sat in an unwritten and unspoken social order as they lived—declining from the front to the rear in the pews of that sanctuary. Those of material and means were in the front, then came the others, the least—the vagrants, the afflicted of body, the broken families, the poorest and thieves of necessity were the endmost of the order to sit. On the back rows they were, the last to come, the first to leave—in the dark places, as they were in life.

Every Sunday the service of communion was offered at ten o'clock in the morning and eight o'clock in the evening. Invitations to the rail, a place which separated the altar, the holy place, from the sinners. They came to kneel on pads of leather. Attached and rising from these pads was the wood lattice work, the stanchions that supported the rail topped also with pads. Covered with fine

red velvet, these supported the arms, the clasped hands, and the weight of bodies with bowed heads of its visitors. Unblemished and pristine no more was this place of suffering, supplication, and sacrament. The richness of this royal velvet also suffered; many spots interrupting the glory of its intention covered it. Moisture, not from a leaking roof, but from leaking hearts, drowning in despair ... tears that fell from the overflowing reservoir of emotions.

Brass. The final piece of the rail was flat and narrow, affixed on the inside just below the armrests, seen only from above by those who knelt and by those who served the sacrament. A temporary receptacle was this thin metallic shelf for the small thimble size glasses from which they drank, for coins, and also envelopes. Small in size were these envelopes, found on the back of the pews. For contributions was their intended purpose, but now, a different purpose they served; not of giving but with notes of spiritual requests and worldly help of any kind.

Habit. The reason formed in his past for attending and participating in church services. Now, there would be other reasons also: reasons of need, dire need, not of spirituality but of physical mortality—financial sustenance. Those of money and means always attended the morning services as there was personal risk when venturing out after nightfall: darkness was the companion of beggars and thieves. And the banker preferred the warmth of the day and its light that shown through the arched windows of the sanctuary. It gave clarity to that place and the people, and the rail. Come Sunday, there would be another reason he came. It was two days after Friday: pay day. Indeed, these times were severe, but there were those who had good fortune of employment, others with savings or inheritance; they possessed money. The devout Christian always gave regardless of amount. There were also others above the suffering ones, who gave but did so as they were expected. Not from the basis of their faith and belief, but only as a process: the part of "going to church." The Sunday Christian. Because of their dress, he knew them. He would observe them, what place at the rail they knelt, and what they gave: coins—pennies, nickels, dimes, and quarters. No envelopes. He would watch. He would wait. He would also go to the rail—but he was now a poor banker, not a beggar.

The sacrament. Bread, broken. Wine, consumed from a common cup by all, was from the fermentation of grapes. Alcohol. Many in history considered it the liquid that dissolved and deleted reason and innocence and created destruction, poverty, despair, and misery. Grape juice cometh. A discovery by those of strict abstinence, through pasteurization, had been substituted for wine. In this church and others, the life created by these times affected also those who served. The priests. Not in the services, but before and after they drank. Official orders, decrees came from the bishop. The practice was to be stopped—changed. The liquid to be served would be the unfermented, the grape juice. But not from the one, the common cup, but the small thimble-sized glasses. From large trays they were given in the tiny cups; after consumption they were left on the rail. But why not from the common cup? Fear was the reason. Diphtheria and tuberculosis. Grape juice of the Eucharist signified, represented the blood of the Christ served by Him just before He died. In this church, it would become the banker's link to living....

Beyond furtive, the magic of abomination would be his method; analysis through observation of those who went before him and whether something came from their pockets, resulted in the when and where he would go—to that rail. His pockets were always bare except he would carry several of those small white envelopes and a handkerchief.

As he approached, being sure there were others kneeling, he would quickly look only at the contents held by the brass; empty cups, envelopes, and coins. He would choose his place by the color of these coins—silver: nickels, dimes, and quarters. And at times he had no choice as the only ones were not silver but copper. Kneeling, a priest served first the small piece of bread, then another followed with the tray containing the small glasses of the purple grape juice. Choosing one of these with his right hand after eating the bread, he would quickly drink. With deliberation, touch, and moving, he always left some of the juice on his lips. Then with his left hand, two and sometimes three fingers, he would wipe them across his wet lips. As this hand dropped toward the rail, with his right hand he took a handkerchief from his pocket and began wiping his mouth.

The left hand, the fingers being moist and sticky, was pressed firmly, unnoticed on the coins—he preferred dimes; size, weight, and amount. He continued this manual ballet as if a pirouette falling, the synchrony of movements of handkerchiefed right hand down and over, covering the left and coins stuck with a temporary glue of the grape juice moved together. Squeezing and wiping off the coins into the handkerchief, it went quickly into his pocket. This act was not over. Before rising, he reached in another pocket and placed one of those small white envelopes on the rail. On the front was written *IOU 25 cents. A friend.* This was the amount taken the previous week. This was not stealing; it was borrowing, a loan.

He was a banker. He lived and would continue to do so by the letter of its monetary written law: a loan required repayment. And always a signature and promise were required. This was his justification—by what was written. The ink, words, and paper were neuter. Emotions, feelings, and opinions were never present. By law. Yet the church had laws also, far beyond those of man; they were written and existed from Eternal laws of Spirit. From deities to despots, they would eventually rule ... virtuous. The Spirit would not satisfy the physiology of hunger. The coins answered. Five cents would buy a can of beans, a container of processed meat, a loaf of bread, or a bowl of soup with endless crackers. A quarter purchased disconnected solace—a bottle of wine—not from the stores, however. Prohibition. But it always could be had as easily as taking a breath—and exhaling a quarter ... the black market had everything. He would tell no one of his method and its reward. No one knew. Already there were too many parasites that lived from these "labors" of others, all dressed as people.

One week passed. No sign of the contractor. The next Sunday the banker went to church and waited almost to the end of the service before participating. He paid little attention to those in the rear; he knew all that they left were the envelopes with requests and prayers for help. Most had already departed. Approaching the gate that separated the left from the right side, he noticed the right side was filled with kneeling worshipers. He turned left and went near the end of the rail. No coins, only envelopes. Waiting for the priest to serve, he looked down at the envelopes; one was different, slightly thicker. Looking closer, he saw the thickness was caused by coins: larger ones. Quarters? Half dollars? Hunger from a day and a half, triggered his method into action, somewhat different but with the same results of possession. While he was drinking from the cup, he placed his handkerchief over this envelope, and with his other hand removed not one, but two of those small envelopes from his pocket. Looking at both of them, he shuffled the two and looking again, chose one and placed it on the rail. An act of distraction to those who might be watching....

With his left hand back on the handkerchief, he clutched and squeezed, compressing and folding the coin containing envelope, causing it to disappear into the cloth. Lifting it quickly he wiped the juice from his lips and finally deep into his pocket it went. Walking quickly down the center aisle, as he approached the large door to the world, he turned back to look, to see if anyone was watching or purposely following. He saw only the candlelit brightness of the grandeur from the altar. The Spirit remained at the rail....

No stores were open on Sunday. Almost torture was the feeling from hunger. But now he had money and there were people who sold things on the streets. Everything. At places where many people passed on the corners there was always one who stood behind a folding wooden tray—selling apples—five cents. He stopped, retrieved the crumpled envelope, and tore open the end, and three coins fell into his hand: a nickel, a quarter, and a half dollar. On one side of the envelope he noticed writing. It read: *The Bible tells me so*. It was signed: *Mary M.* Yes, he remembered that the Bible did say many things and one was to help the lesser, yet he did not complete and process the depth of its entirety. He was in need and had been helped—through his own devious ways that were created by so many things and so many other people—he was one of the multitudes—a victim. His rationalization. With a fleeting mental thank you, he tore the small envelope into tiny pieces and threw them down on the street. Then, the largest apple. A nickel. The first bite of sweetness. He returned to the shelter. A seventy-five cent Monday would begin his week....

The next morning dawned and what with it came to him a temporary security that would last until the next Sunday—what seventy-five cents would buy. One block from the food store he saw a woman and two children selling sandwiches—cheese and bread only—for five cents. This "dinner meal" would keep until evening when he made his next visit to the yard, hoping for the return of the contractor. He gave the woman his quarter—she had no change. After going into a nearby pharmacy she returned—a sandwich and two dimes she handed him. Carefully putting the sandwich in his coat pocket and crossing the street to the store, he noticed her—a small woman, holding a bag, looking down. As he came closer, he saw what apparently had happened; something had fallen from the bag and broken. It was a glass jar that had been filled with vegetables and thick liquid—stew—homemade and canned, from those now forced to sell this and other items in these stores. Five cents for one quart they received. The store owners then resold—ten cents they received. The ledge of poverty was becoming more narrow.... There were other things on the ground, things that she had scavenged, but no food. Her knit bag had split, now useless to carry these items. She would not be able to handle this task she was attempting: to pick up, hold, and carry. Not speaking, he gathered these things and asked if he could help. Yes, thank you, did he mind? With no money left, she would go home.

It was only a few blocks to her house in an area that seemed out of place—a block of older structures, not destroyed, eaten, and swallowed, taken over by the constant appetite of growth. Most of the inhabitants were widows—pensioners of the government. When he opened the door of her house, he noticed that it would not close completely. Jammed. It could not be locked, and worse, the cold of the season could not be kept out. Inside, he placed her items on the table, one of the few pieces of furniture there—stark in design and appearance, but functional—military surplus. He could see in the small kitchen with its open shelves—empty except for a small bag of flour. A coffee pot on the stove. Next to it, a sink with a dripping faucet. Some coffee? It was still warm she said, as the iron stove remained hot long after the fire had gone out. No sugar or cream—once staples, now rare delicacies. He sat at the table, arranging those things he had just placed while she was preparing the coffee. Black and bitter it was, but warm, the important part. They sat. They talked of these times, their histories, and finally what had caused their meeting: the jar that was no more, broken— feeding nothing.... Until her government check would arrive in three days, that stew would have lasted. But she had experienced meager happenings such as this one in the past. Before anything, the hunger must be quelled, replaced by food, the fuel for energy—now, profoundly, just to survive. After an hour passed, he felt her hunger. He reached in his pocket and withdrew the wrapped sandwich and gave it to her, smiling, and telling her he hoped it would help—at least for this day. She gave it back, thanking him for this gesture, and saying how kind it was for him but—he needed it. He insisted. A game of refusal. A stalemate. Relenting, she took the sandwich into the kitchen and returned with two small plates; she had cut it into halves. Surprised, he listened as she said if one is in need, then there is need for sharing. Picking up his half, beginning to eat, she stopped him; a blessing she offered, for this day, for these times, for the two of them, and for all who suffered. Cheese, bread, and coffee—a feast for any pauper....

Finished, preparing to depart, he extended his hand to hers—she instead opened her arms and embraced him. Clasped hands would not have been gratitude enough for their fortuitous meeting and destiny ... something that was beyond their present physical selves. Requiring extra strength to open the door, he looked at it closely—a hinge had come loose and dislodged, causing the door to tilt, preventing closure. He would return to repair: an offering she accepted. And she had a box of tools with nails, screws, and other necessary things; they were her late husband's. Exchanging smiles, gracious gratitudes, and goodbyes, they parted.

Ten minutes to the store. After buying a can of beans, with sixty-five cents left in his pocket, he walked rapidly to the yard. Upon his arrival, people had already begun to gather. He mingled among them, searching. No contractor. Going to that place in the corner, he saw the sign with its rusting rails. He would trespass there again.

Remembering that first fire, he began: pieces of wood, arranged in a square. A loud laugh surprised him, looking up, he had returned: this contractor, this builder. How quickly this banker had become "a frontiersman" were the contractor's words. The pocket knife, the beans, and now two spoons ... prosperity—they ate. They talked of the past days; the contractor had followed the thief but was unable to apprehend him. The banker told of his encounter with a little woman and her travails. With the next day coming and as always nothing on their "schedule," they would go to restore that door.

The next morning, she answered their knock. After introducing the contractor, the three sat for a cup of that coffee; it was different — in temperature only, as the fire in that stove still burned. Then came the repairs, but before they began, the box of tools she brought from a closet. The contractor's eyes sparkled when he saw them. There were more than needed for almost any building and repairing.

First the leaking faucet yielded to the turning of a wrench; a window latch, a loose light switch connection. Last, the front door required more time and effort. Realigning the hinge and resetting the door, then opening and closing from the inside and out, they restored its operation. Clapping her hands and letting out a gleeful squeal, the little woman opened, closed, opened, and closed it. To these two men, her happiness was satisfactory payment for their work. Before leaving, they looked throughout the house; there was more to be done: fixed, repaired, and restored. They would return again. But next door, across the street ... eyes. They closed the door, down the steps on the path to the street they walked. Curiosity followed them, those eyes of the people in the nearby houses— widows, and some with children.

With a renewed, but a different kind of energy, the two came back to that neighborhood, to her house. Finishing outside, the loose screens covering all of the windows were firmly reattached. Just after midday they went inside to begin the remaining task of the interior. They saw her in the kitchen, over the stove, stirring a pot. She came out followed by something known only to the olfactory of experience: an aroma that told stories—stew. It was Friday; two days after the government check. The store. Another jar, carried with success to its worthy serving. And simple biscuits from that bag of flour.

As they were walking away from the house, a woman came from a nearby dwelling and stopped them. She had noticed what these two men had been doing and asked if they could look and perhaps repair her front door also. She could pay them for their services, she said. Observing the door from the street, it appeared to suffer the same odd tilt and alignment as did their original project. Yes, tomorrow they would return and repair the door—and more.

Arriving the next morning with the borrowed tools, they began with the door but saw inside almost the identical problems as the first they encountered. Their payment: a loaf of bread, a nickel, thank yous, and, yes, a telling embrace for each man. Their acts were not over with this house....

Over the next days, and into the next week it continued: requests, almost pleading, from other widows in other houses, were fulfilled by these two, this odd combination of builder and banker. Their remuneration, sometimes beyond food and coins—a shirt, a coat, or other usable items of value they were given. The excess of these things they took to the shelter, to the yard, to be shared.

In the second week of their work, as they were finishing for the day, they saw it approaching: a land leviathan with wheels, a black Packard automobile. Stopping beside them, the back door of the car opened, and a man of business appearance emerged. He also was a banker. The president of one of the few that had survived in this large city; common conservative sense and concern for its customers' security were the reasons. The Packard's passenger questioned the nature, the purpose, and what these two were doing. The two told him of their pasts; the yard, the shelter, all, to this present day—results of the continuing depression. Beyond the depths of the apparent and the unspoken, was something that supported it all: the motivation of man to achieve and receive beyond physical reward—spiritual perpetuation of the soul's being.

Opening the car door and preparing to leave, he told them that his bank now owned this block, these houses. They were purchased from the government as it was rapidly reducing all unnecessary burdens; those considered expendable. Demolition of the block would begin in the early spring, later to become a site of modern concrete and steel: buildings of business—not of residence. But what would become of those who now lived there? It was not his bank's problem—the government was "researching a solution of relocation." Until notified, these two could continue their work. The two accepted an offer of transportation, and the car carried the three to the yard.

Only a few noticed as the men got out of the car; their concerns were of the moment, the coming night, and what tomorrow's hours would hold. Shaking hands and thanking him, the two with food from the day's labors went to their unoccupied place. The man and the Packard remained ... many minutes of directed observation and thought he had of this place, these people, and these two men. They were an enigma of directed devotion, without reservations....

Into the first week of December it continued: from house to house they toiled for those who did not know of the fate that would come with the spring time. On the Saturday two weeks before Christmas, the black Packard came again—the second visit from the new owner. The notification? The car door opened and, emerging without words, from banker to banker a letter was exchanged. Written to the local hardware store were instructions to give these two men any materials they requested; the statement of costs to be credited and paid by this bank—now an outpost of survival that opened its gates. The block, the houses, and the people would remain; it would be revitalized if they agreed. And they would be paid.

Because of what these two were giving to those whose needs seemed so basic, this banker realized that the future survival was in the people who suffered and those who helped—not in destroying and rebuilding inert structures. His bank also had purchased the yard and the failed factory. A generous amount, not to be bought for the tax liens that gave nothing to those who once possessed the property, but instead to the owners and workers it was given. Its vision of resurrection would later be realized. The notification was more than enough to continue their manual efforts; it was also mankind's spring time of the stored energy to come forth from the warmth of spiritual compassion and care. The three would meet many times again.

Watching the car slowly depart on the snowy street, with disbelief replaced by elation, they returned to where it all began: to her front door, an opening once broken and restored, just as their lives and many other lives had been and would be. She had been watching from a window, this meeting of men, and opening the door, invited them in. Coffee? Yes, they sat and she returned—with sugar and cream! It was beyond benevolence and generosity of the story she heard. As they were leaving, she asked a favor of the now employed banker. Her arthritis had gone deeper just as the snow, and she would not be able to walk to the Sunday church services. Would he take her monthly envelope? Leave it at the rail? It was the same church; puzzled in thought, he said yes. He had never seen her there, as with most of her lot, he was not concerned—no attention was given to them. Putting the envelope in his pocket, they departed.

The church bells tolled at ten o'clock the next morning, that Sunday. Thinking only of that worldly pot of gold, received yesterday, and not the storm that brought the rainbow, he went to the rail. Waiting for the priests to serve, he took the envelope she had given him from his pocket and placed it on the rail. Something was written on it: *The Bible tells me so. Mary M.* As if the first unanticipated rumble of an earthquake and accompanying storms, unexpected shock consumed him. Beyond self-anger and uncontrolled shame, the immorality of his conduct and his disgrace through the iniquity of his transgressions seized him. Diametric this was—rapture reversed. The Spirit, just as he did as a banker, through Heavenly tolerance, from the celestial coffers, had made this man a loan of goodness. And now it was being called to be repaid. This grace period had ended, but another embodiment of Grace would prevent foreclosure, the foreclosure of this man's soul. It began with tears coming from the wellspring of man's physical mortality, the heart. Unknown love, would be the lethality of his self-deception. Sealing the instant renegotiations of this loan

were silent prayers asking for forgiveness—God always listens and promises. The rainbow appeared....

The priests served; he ate, he drank. Words of the hymn playing he heard,

Be thou my vision...
Heart of my own heart,
whatever befall,
Still be my vision,
O Ruler of all.

Walking out of the church, the bells in its steeple rang, "Adeste Fidelis." Christmas, more than that of yesterday, a gift of the season, just realized and received at that rail, and the bells caused a compassionate collision of his heart and the Spirit. The cold of that snowy day surrounded him, but he was warm. The next day, a letter to his wife he sent. Of all he told except the secret of the envelopes and the rail; known only but for two.

Christmas Day. She had invited the two "new businessmen" but they agreed only if they were allowed to bring the holiday food. Just after noon they arrived and she was silently surprised when she saw they carried nothing. Having been in that house for only a short time, there was a knock at the door. The contractor opened it; a man standing holding a large steaming metal pan with thick gloves said, "Merry Christmas." She immediately went to the door, and after thanking him, asked who had sent it. "Santa Claus," he replied and quickly left. She looked out of the open door and saw several trucks with men delivering to each house. Christmas dinners. Her two guests laughed softly. They knew. The future, as with the first Christmas, began on that Christmas Day.

As winter passed into spring, this foundling business began to grow as did the surroundings of nature. With enough saved and a journey to his wife and children arranged, the banker spent a week on his wife's family farm in the early summer. A reunion of remembrance. But he had to return to that city, that company as his business skills were required in those still crucial times. His family understood and accepted, knowing that no promise was needed of when he would return, an inevitability. On his return, he stopped in the city that he had left. And the bank. Still closed, but inside people were there, sorting through its past, its mistakes, and possible future. Eventually, with federal protection, it would live again.

The remaining days of the summer and fall were filled with accelerated action of their work, these three, and always first were the people in the greatest, the most dire need. The shelter was more than refurbished, it was enlarged: dormitories, baths, and a new kitchen; a place that provided, a place that never denied. The yard and factory would become the site, the center for those who once slept there, now employed in its function: to go out, these Samaritans of service, to those places to those people. The block of houses was not to be demolished but renovated for efficiency and comfort for those times; all accomplished giving a healthy newness in the ordination of living civility. This company, born of man's destitution, would grow to build, to give with foremost, the foundations that sustain life: security, concern, care, and compassion.

The second Christmas would come, and with reservation and forced encouragement, for a week to the family farm he would travel—this time by rail, a gift from the other two of the trio. Yet he would return, driven by an inner sense of his blemished being to continue the labors of the seemingly insurmountable conditions.

Visions of the imagined of those impoverished were transformed and manifested into wishes granted. And of that house, the home, hers, in January it would begin: the first to be completely uplifted—a new life to it would come. But her emphatic wish that all others come first, before hers, would be granted.

Five days after Christmas, returning and carrying that same suitcase, the short mile he walked on that familiar street. He smiled as he passed the first few of these that would soon become "new" homes. Into view, he saw hers, but in front, a blur of blackness—a car and something larger: a hearse. His heart began to quicken, his steps slowed. No. On the door, a white wreath hung. Inside were suited men of the mortuary and several neighbors, and in a corner, the two. The day after Christmas she had passed away, they told him—a new white handkerchief he withdrew from his pocket. Her service, the next day in that church, would be held; she would rest next to her husband.

Not going to, as Moses did, but coming to her, this new Canaan she only saw. Her house would not become one of the others, the one to complete this oasis, but the only one to remain in the land that once waited for its spring time. Just as it was on the day she died, it would be preserved as a historical site of national significance, a museum for generations to visit—to experience.

This place of perseverance was beginning to be experienced elsewhere as the benevolent disease of positive progress spread— the city, the country, the world. Months would become years before the strength of stability matured, giving those who once wandered the direction of renewed living. And, after almost two years with the soundness of normalcy returning, these three parted.

The contractor and the banker of benefaction would remain to continue to build, to give. The one from the South would go back to his family, a new home—and the bank he left. He would raise it up just as they did those houses and their inhabitants he was leaving. Becoming its president, in name, action, and unspoken consultation with the Spirit, he would always be sure that its doors were open to all—never tilted or jammed....

And in the years to come, just before Christmas, he would always return to that city in the North, not by bus, but by shiny steel rails. Going to that church, dressed in disguise, in the same clothes he first wore, from the back row to the rail he would walk. He carried one of those small envelopes which contained continued repayment of that first loan. Not coins or requests but an anonymous cashier's check of thousands. Written on it was: *The Bible tells me so. A friend (and Mary M)*.

The Great Depression. Some say it started in a bank, in the South. But to those who read this story, perhaps it may be said the beginning of its end was that Christmas, in that place; from the eternal Spirit's stored Grace was its inception, born of the rail and envelopes....

The Christmas Chalice

"I"... In the first person this story will be told. From my presence, observations, participation, from others, and in the vernacular you will know it. Its ancestry began in the manger, in Bethlehem, and this beginning led to a mortal end, and this triumphant end was mankind's eternal beginning. Close to one hundred years ago it was....

CONSCRIPTION. The compulsory law of the nation. He was twenty-two years old, drafted into military service in the summer of 1917 to cross the sea, to fight in "The Great War," "The War to End All Wars"—World War I. And in December of that year, he had been at the front, in France, for two months. A stalemate. Back and forth, separated by "no man's land," they fought and they died. On Christmas Eve of that year, his life was changed forever.

In early March, it arrived: a letter to his home, his family—his mother. It read:

My Dearest Mother,

Please know that my life continues through the longest days in a land that once was a modern Eden. It is of colors no more, and its gentle contours now are transformed into craters, and it is a sanctum of extinction that would revolt even Satan himself: a place more than nothingness. You may recognize this letter is not of my pen, for my hands have been injured and the holding of objects cannot be. A nurse, Aceline, transcribes what you now read. I, as well as other wounded ones, am in her gentle care. She is from the south of France, and for three long years she has labored here for the broken bodies, for the broken spirits. A gentle smile and touch she gives to those who survive; tears and prayers for those who live no more. She ruffles at my words, only saying it is not her work but God's. Silent affirmations I give in return.

Christmas here was only another day so much like all the others of war. Yet when I think of you, Pa, and baby sister Louise, of home, and of all that which for us was a joyous time, I am lifted from this wasteland of the forsaken: memories....
My fondest of all was the Christmas Eve when Louise was only six years old; of the manger figurines and the chalice, that Christmas Chalice. Oh, Ma, that night was extraordinary, beyond the imagined, truly of Christmas and the blessings that continue to be given because of God's Gift. Do you remember

that night? Aceline wants to know of it, so I shall relive it for her as she writes and smiles for you.

Pa's Christmas gift to us that year was the manger scene that he secretly carved. Everything. Shepherds, sheep, oxen, donkeys, the Wise Men, Mary, Joseph, and Baby Jesus lying in the cradle. Polished and pristine ... perfect. Then came the story as only Pa could tell it: why Christmas was, is, and forever will be of man's continuing journey, temporary here, eternal there.

But it was the Christmas Chalice, that cup, that was the center of it all. A vessel that has existed for how long and its origin, I know not. Always on Christmas Eve it was filled with hot cocoa made with rich milk, and all would drink, passing it slowly to each other as Pa would lovingly speak. And on that Christmas Eve it happened.... As Louise was passing the cup to me, she tipped it over, spilling the warm liquid on the manger scene. She began to cry; she had ruined the beautiful gift, she said. As we tried to console her and dry everything, she said no; she would do it, clean it, as she had caused it. Gently and carefully, through her tears, she restored the soaked figures as if nothing had ever touched them ... except one small place.

On the mouth of Baby Jesus she left a small bit, a dot of that chocolate. When I told her she had missed that, she said no, she had not. Why? Because Jesus was a person just like she was, and He would like chocolate too. She understood in a child's world that God had created man and Jesus in His own image ... and chocolate.

Aceline stopped writing; she was smiling and wiping away tears. Joy from a soaring heart, manifesting itself in unseen feelings. Enter the Spirit.... A pat on his cheek and "Merci, merci," it was time to replace the bandages on his injured hands. For a time they had to stop writing for this medical task. After his wounds were cleansed and new wrappings placed, they resumed this happy time ... reliving. Aceline was immersed in not only hearing, translating, and writing, out of the story to be written, but also in events of such proportions that were not beyond belief but were Belief.

Another page would complete this letter that was to be sent home to his family. But the censors, those who read, who removed parts, or left that which was written, must first and last be involved. Nothing could be written or sent that might reveal any information that could be of aid to the enemy. During wartime, mail was intercepted by spies. This second, this last page, was not destroyed but was returned privately to Aceline as it contained "sensitive" things. The censor who read and reviewed it was so taken, and so shaken, by its words, said it must be saved and revealed. He told her that she would know "when it was time."

Four weeks later, this one-page letter, with the censored page removed, arrived at the soldier's home. Relief and gladness overflowed. They would await further news. But none came. Several months passed. Then, in early summer it arrived; not a letter but a telegram. The dreaded telegram. "We regret to inform you ... " was the usual opening line, the introduction to the end of someone's life. But this one, rare and beautiful, said, "Your son is alive. Moved to area of rehabilitation, recuperation, and rest. Updates to follow." A reprieve to anticipated sadness was the immediate consolation, yet anguish and apprehension were still felt and unspoken. Total obliteration of this fear would only, could only happen upon the ultimate—his return. Days and weeks passed. Nothing. Waiting. A mailbox of wanting, but never receiving the desires, the answers to pleas from man to God.

In early September, a knock on the door: the postman, smiling. In his hand, a letter with a stamp of many colors, from another land. France. The script of Aceline. In it, she apologized for the time that had passed, but assured that all was well with their beloved son. Soon after the Christmas letter, a tragedy had struck: her father was lost, killed in the war, and she had to leave to attend to all that accompanies death. She left abruptly, telling him, her favorite soldier of all, that she would return. A bond she would not break. She ended the letter, saying only that their son was still recuperating and she would keep them informed of his health.

What she did not tell his family was that, upon her return to the hospital, at first sight, she found the same soldier yet something was different. She recognized him but did not know him. Distant. Changed. Then she saw it, or the absence of it—his right arm. Shortly after she had left, complications had set in from his wounds. Infection. Gangrene. Amputation. Unable to cope with the present and to comprehend his future, and without her care and loving support, he had also lost normal connections to life. From melancholy to misery, he spiraled downward into despondency in thought and expression. With this reversal of seeming progress and well-being, he was now on the precipice of falling into a chasm of physical and mental wreckage. Already there were far too many as he, who had followed a predictable road, who were returned and placed in these "convalescent" hospitals, better known as asylums, for continued "recovery" ... never to leave. Prisoners of walls and enslaved by their own minds, they were not living—only existing.

For him, the standard protocol was tried again and again with no improvement. "Combat stress reaction" and "shell shock" it was called.... Orders were prepared to send him home, to one of those "places." Only a week remained before his departure, his "deportation" from normalcy. Nothing was left, nothing else could be done ... of this nurse and her soldier, their bond would be severed. A few days of monotony were all that existed. She pleaded: allow her more time to try, to attempt, to endeavor to bring him back into some semblance of living. Thanking her for her concern, the official answer was no, as his place in the hospital was needed for more incoming wounded. Overwhelming and catastrophic was this final decision. Her reaction did not go unnoticed ... nor unfelt. You may take him, they said, along with others of his condition, to—she stopped listening as she knew of this small village. In the mountains only a half-day's train ride it was: a place of guest houses, a small hotel, a café, simple homes, and a church. A holiday and vacation spot in peace, it had become a haven of escape and solitude for the broken ones of war. There they would go, the soldiers and their attendants, the caretakers of what remained of once whole men. There was word throughout, not official, of this place, that something special was there, outwardly unknown, but felt ... send them there, those who had little left to lose; one last experience for the senses, or a new beginning of the spirit.

The passenger cars were filled; all were in uniform, some in white, the soldiers in their summer cotton dress of light brown. Some walked unaided, others with crutches and canes, and a few in special chairs to be carried or rolled. Conversation was subdued as everyone's attention was consumed by the vistas of the land and its beauty; the world as it should be, absent of the devastation of war. Upon arrival, the soldiers were settled in their guest rooms and would rest the remainder of the afternoon. A dinner for them would be held in the hotel with local musicians and singers as entertainment.

The afternoon would allow Aceline the time needed to finalize her one last effort to save and prevent his loss to the land of no-return. A plan she would implement. She knew the most essential part of the salvaging and deliverance protocol, the return to life, was the restoration of belief, of and in himself. But she needed help, a companion who had knowledge and experience of these human complexities that reached far beyond the physical—to the soul. She realized she would need only a few answers, nothing more, as her knowledge provided the anchor for the lifeline of rescue. She went to the church—the priest.... After an hour of conversation passed with the soldier's history being told, the priest graciously agreed to do his part. He had seen many similar situations, but not quite such as this one. He was silently confident that he could give renewed sustenance for the soldier's lost belief and spirit. Acceptance of this "panis angelicus," this bread of angels, must come from the soldier's heart.

That evening, the banquet with wonderful food, the entertainment, and the intermittent camaraderie were partial affirmations of the positive; the physical results of this gathering. Concern still remained for those detached from any emotion, merely attending as if they were enduring and not enjoying the experience. Her soldier was one of those, yet she felt he still possessed some unmanifested self-control that kept the finality of destruction at bay. But what was it? The journey from the hospital and the evening's festivities fatigued the guests and they were secured in their rooms for the night. The next day had no organized activities and all would be free to go, to do as they wished.

After a late breakfast, they were ready for a walk up to an overlook. A site seen by many it was, in person and the world over through picture postcards. Inspired by its panorama and beauty, she took him there. Not speaking, they sat. Watching him, she waited, hoping for his verbal response. Nothing. No words. An inner fear gripped her. Then she glanced at his face, his eyes.... He was looking at, not through or beyond as it usually seemed, but now focused. Concentrated and absorbed he was. To that valley, those mountains, and all that was before them, his eyes went. Minutes turned into a half hour. He stood.... "Beautiful," he said. The sound of that word resonated with meaning to her. Exhilaration. Beyond the singularity of it was a connection, an attachment to the world, to her, and to himself. Then, looking down, in a monotonous whisper, he said, "We must go." The distant stare returned and mechanical in his walking, he turned and started down the hill. Holding hands, side by side, they returned to the village. Pointing toward the church, she suggested they go there. He silently obliged.

Upon entering the church, he came to a halt, to attention, in military style. The bright sun shone through the stained-glass windows, with the streams of color in an exactness, undeviating until they were stopped by whatever objects they reached. He did not move, but his eyes did. Surveying its entirety, he began slowly walking toward the front, to the altar. She quickly caught up to him, clasping his hand once again. Through a side door, he entered: the priest. He was a man much more in age than the two visitors, in a long black robe with a high collar, the traditional dress for those servants. From the many afflicted he had encountered, he learned not to ask questions, but rather to gently, in a soft and caring voice, talk only of this place, this church. He directed his speech to the both of them so as not to create any indication or insinuation to the soldier of attempts, of interference, or forced direction which could have dire or irreversible consequences to his fragile state.

Through the church they went, hearing of its history, seeing, and touching its relics. Then outside, to the careful order of the grounds. Flowers, plants, and trees adorned its exterior; nature's invitation to visit. They returned to the front, to the steps leading to the large open doors. The soldier said nothing but went back to the entrance. Standing immobile, looking in once again, he was drawn to those beams of light....

As evening approached, the air became cooler. The three walked across the small town square to the café for a warming drink. They sat in the front, in a corner around a small table. The owner saw them, nodded, and went through the swinging doors to the kitchen. He was also prepared for his duty. Several minutes later, he returned with a tray holding three cups. Steaming, they were placed carefully in front of the three. The soldier sat fixed, gazing forlornly out of the window with unknown thoughts traveling on an unseen path into his mental wilderness. Then, he turned quickly toward the other two; something had caught his attention. A smell of unique sweetness ... chocolate! Hot chocolate! His face, still unchanged, but the eyes now bright, had signaled to his companions that a crack through the impenetrable had occurred. And the cup in front of him was different than the other two plain white ones. His was of colors. He looked closely at it: a Christmas cup. He slowly lifted and softly touched the edge of that cup to his lips; tasting its contents, then lowering the cup, a gentle smile appeared on his face. He looked at the two of them and said, "Home." Tears came from Aceline's eyes; the priest said nothing, only smiling as he had seen such happenings in the past.

The conversation slowly began. This cup of hot chocolate triggered the displaced memories: of the letter written home months ago, the telling of Christmas Eve there, the Christmas Chalice, filled with, yes, hot chocolate. But then he stopped; he could remember no more. Something had happened before, on that battlefield, on that last Christmas Eve that blocked his memory. Tangled with his injuries, it took him into that deranged darkness of his mind to this present time; the absence of caring ... life.

"You will know when it is time." Aceline remembered the censor's words and knew that time was at hand. She took the page from her pocket, explained to the soldier what it was, why she possessed it, and all that had occurred since that last Christmas Eve on that battleground.

Carefully and slowly she would read, and with the priest, observe and be prepared for his reactions, both visual and spoken. They would be patient, pause, answer any questions from him, and lovingly support him during the most crucial moments that were to come. They would go with him, from the mystery to the point of solution from which he would begin to live again.

She began to read that second page ....

> *Christmas Eve here, only a month past, was dire, yet the time of an encounter, unexpected, from the desperate to which may have been the divine. I truly do not know or understand all of it. At two o'clock in the afternoon, we were ordered to advance on the German lines, only one hundred yards through barbed wire, machine guns, and deep shell holes. Up the ladder, out of the trench we went, men falling, men advancing. Then it came; artillery shells began to drop. One landed nearby, sending me skyward. Smoke, fire, and earth; all in an erupting*

cyclone of force with a mixing of men and matter of war; with ruination and death as their only destination.

I awoke in blackness and quiet. Night. Strange, no more explosions. At the far end of that shell hole were two soldiers: one from my unit, one from the enemy. Motionless, with meaningless moaning, they were alive. My arms and hands had begun to awaken. Pain—I closed my eyes, drifting, floating. Then, the smell: sausage! Ma, you know how Pa and I love sausage and this, although foreign, was familiar. Was I in Heaven? No, the Germans, only a short distance away, were cooking and singing. It was their Christmas Eve also.

Still, no explosions. Why? Carefully crawling to the top of the crater, I looked toward the enemy lines. White flags. Had they surrendered? Was the war over? I turned and looked back to the place from whence I had come just hours before. There were white flags there also. A truce. A respite. No more killing. A man-made miracle. A gift of life, exchanged between those who hated one another. I prayed ....

Sliding back down to the bottom of that hole, I heard the two soldiers again, coughing with groans of agony. They became quiet again; then one reached over and touched the hand of the other. The one he touched, the one from my unit, began to sing in a clear and perfectly pitched voice:

"Pass me not o' gentle Savior,
Hear my humble cry.
While on others Thou art calling
Do not pass me by."

Upon hearing this, all noise from the enemy trenches stopped. Then his voice began to weaken, he sang no more. A cough; he began again, the verses mixed and broken—

"Let me at Thy throne of mercy
Find a sweet relief."

Pausing, his last words:
"Save me by Thy Grace."

Then, nothing.... I listened; a soft lingering sigh came. The hymn and the soldier finished. I prayed.
    Slowly, the German, lying beside him, raised his arm and began to sing:

"Stille Nacht, heilge Nacht
Alles schläft; einsam wacht."

I knew not the words, but the music, yes: "Silent Night, Holy Night." He sang until he, too, stopped with the same gentle sigh, then no more; truly, all was calm. Then from the German trenches, the carol continued. Of baritones and angelic altos, their voices combined, sent a cloud of spiritual velvet across that field of death. I cried. I closed my eyes. When I opened them again, a stream of brilliant light, as thin as a violin string, from above as distant as I could see, slowly came down. I waited for the explosion or clap of thunder, but there was no sound. The light stopped between the two soldiers nearby. It became larger, just enough to cover them.

Illuminating their entirety, almost blinding it was. Then in a second, I felt a gentle breeze and that light, now at its brightest, as quickly as it came, disappeared into the star-filled night, into the heavens. I waited, for I did not know if it might return again, this time with vengeance. I must see. I crawled through the mud, the mire, and the stench of that hole to the now still and quiet soldiers. Their bodies bore the results of battle, but their faces were clean and smooth. Their expressions were of contentment, not of agony and pain but of peace. A fragrance, not of that war, but of lilacs, roses, and lilies, lingered: clean, fresh, and pure.

A dream. I closed my eyes again. Waiting. Blinking, it was the same. Everything was the same. To be certain, I crawled back to the top, to the edge, just above the two lifeless soldiers and looked toward the German lines. One of them rose and stood at the top of his trench, his silhouette I could see. He raised his arms, outstretched them upward, and looked into the clear darkness. He shouted—no, he cried—he cried out "Gott bleibt!" That is my last memory of that night, Christmas Eve, as pain returned and carried me into delirium and unconsciousness.

The soldier's lips began to quiver; he swallowed with difficulty, as his head dropped. He made no sound as his cheeks glistened— tears. From that night, all of the fractured parts and pieces were now before him. Not hesitating, Aceline reached over and held his hand; the priest placed his hand on the armless shoulder. The priest began:

"Gott bleibt!" The German's words were telling it all, everything; "God abides."

What you saw, many others have experienced it, yet many have not, even though they may have been next to ones who did. Belief was the difference, the reason that separated those who saw and those who did not. And at that time, you were not alone.

Those of faith and belief in war and in life are never nor will they ever be alone, for God is truly abiding, remaining steadfast with comfort and grace. There have been those in this war, and to be sure on both sides, who have had this happen only to be in that light at a later time. But you did not; you are alive, yet all that has befallen you has left you without aspirations or belief in yourself and what lies beyond your present existence. The vastness of life contains that which we know, that which we can see, and yes, the unknown: the future. And there can be empty destinations in that future. To travel there, without guidance and assurance, can be beyond man's ability to think, to reason what may exist in its barrenness. You have arrived in one of those empty places and for understandable human reasons: loss. You have lost not only comrades, but part of your physical self. Doubt has entered. But if you lose something irreplaceable, God will help you find something greater.

So it is with Christmas: everything we lose in life, even life itself, can be replaced through His Gift. You witnessed that; the light came down to those two soldiers near you on that field of death. From life's exhaustion to exaltation, take yourself, look to His light. And through Christmas that was His Promise ... all you have to do is ask....

On December 24, 1918, a horse-drawn enclosed taxi arrived on a snow-covered street in his town, at his home. He had returned.

They were on the porch: Ma, Pa, and Louise with smiles, and yes, wet eyes. The driver climbed down from his seat and went to the taxi's door. The three on the porch were surprised to see a figure, a woman, emerge from the other side.

There was only one it could be: it was Aceline. The driver opened the door and with their help, he climbed down, dressed in military winter wools. A long overcoat, with the right sleeve pinned to his side, covered him almost to his boots. The driver refused payment, saying it was his honor and privilege to serve those who served him, who served them all. With a "Merry Christmas," he departed. Still outside, embraces, kisses, and smiles ended as they went inside to warmth.

As he took off his great coat, they saw the right sleeve of his tunic was folded neatly, sloping downward, and angled toward his waist, affixed and flattened as it was of military meaning. They stared blankly at this sight, but he released them from their stupor, smiling and saying that his left arm would just do twice as much. Above his heart on his uniform was another heart; one of purple ....

A decorated tree, adorned as never before, was in that room, with candles across the mantle above the burning logs in the great fireplace. A setting from the past, today, and the future it would be.

A cake of fruit was the finale of the meal that gratified, that surpassed its nourishment ... it was the Season. Conversations about the past, not of the war, but of this day and the coming of the morrow were lively; smiles and laughter radiated in abundance. Finished, they arose, gathering around the manger scene. The soldier walked toward it, and with his one hand, reached and grasped my hand(le). The Spirit soared in my soul as I was filled with hot chocolate.

For I, in the first person, I am the Christmas Chalice ... it was Christmas Eve once again.